Step coupling

Step coupling

*Creating and Sustaining
a Strong Marriage
in Today's Blended Family*

SUSAN WISDOM, LPC, and JENNIFER GREEN

THREE RIVERS PRESS • NEW YORK

Authors' Note

When relating the stories of people's lives, one always guards the privacy of those who have shared personal details. That alone would prompt us to use fictitious names for the stepcouples and stepfamilies whose lives we plumb for the keys to success.

Even more caution is needed when discussing stepcouples. They exist in a web of relationships that includes children, ex-spouses, ex-spouses' new partners, and stepsiblings. A slip of the pen could compromise ties that were tenuous to begin with.

To maintain the privacy of the stepcouples and stepfamilies whose stories we tell, we've disguised every significant detail. Ages, occupations, family composition, length of marriage, previous relationships—all have been altered. However, the tales, both encouraging and cautionary, illustrate universal truths about stepcoupling.

Published by Three Rivers Press, New York, New York.
Member of the Crown Publishing Group, a division of Random House, Inc.

www.randomhouse.com

THREE RIVERS PRESS and the Tugboat design are registered trademarks of Random House, Inc.

Printed in the United States of America

Design by Rhea Braunstein

Library of Congress Cataloging-in-Publication Data

Wisdom, Susan.
Stepcoupling : creating and sustaining a strong marriage in today's blended family / Susan Wisdom and Jennifer Green.—1st ed.
Includes bibliographical references.
1. Stepfamilies—United States.   2. Remarried people—United States.
I. Green, Jennifer, 1957–   II. Title.
HQ759.92 W57 2002
306.874—dc21   2001053508

ISBN 0-609-80741-2

10 9 8 7

FIRST EDITION

To love, courage,
and tenacity.

acknowledgments

First, thank you to Amye Dyer of AMG/Renaissance for her enthusiastic, unwavering belief in this book.

Linda Kaplan's early reading of *Stepcoupling* was appreciated, her selfless encouragement a precious gift. Missy Vaux Hall, a dear friend, also read an early version; her generous ear and honest feedback were instrumental. Caren Prentice's steadfast presence counted more than she'll ever know.

Without Jonalyn Wallace, this book would never have been written. Thank you for introducing us to each other and for an early reading, laughter, and light. Jonalyn and Paul also offered critical logistical support: a home away from home, excellent meals, good coffee, and several glasses of wine.

For personal and professional support, thank you to David Freeman, Miriam Resnick, Kathy Mulder, Carolyn Campbell, and Carol McD. Wallace.

Thank you to our children and stepchildren for the gifts and challenges and the soul-searching growth that resulted.

Finally and forever, thank you to David and Randy for belief, patience, and everlasting support.

contents

one

Congratulations! You're Part of a Stepcouple

Annie and Mike sitting in a tree
K-I-S-S-I-N-G
First comes love
Then comes marriage
Then comes Annie with a baby carriage.

A stereotypical first marriage follows the rhyme. A wedding comes after romance, and babies arrive later. Lovers ease into family life, adding children over a period of years.

Unfortunately, for every two weddings celebrated in a given year, a divorce becomes final. And within five years of divorcing, 89 percent of men and 79 percent of women walk down the aisle again.

Second—or third or even fourth—marriages refute the rhyme. First come Mike and Annie pushing baby carriages. Love and a wedding follow, and the happy, harried couple sneaks k–i–s–s–i–n–g in when the kids aren't looking.

The scrambled verse describes *stepcoupling*.★ Adults get to know each other and build a healthy relationship while adjusting to, and combining, existing families.

★This word captures the unique ongoing process of forming and maintaining a marriage when children are involved. It also focuses squarely on the adults, as opposed to the stepfamily or stepchildren.

It happens all the time. In the mid-1990s, one in three Americans was a stepparent, a stepchild, a stepsibling, or some other member of a stepfamily. Some predict that by the year 2007, stepfamilies will outnumber nuclear families.

Stepcouples face stresses that first couples don't: children (his, hers, and theirs), financial support of two or more households, custody and legal issues, and biological parents outside the home. Value conflicts and different parenting styles turn up the heat.

Statistics tell the story best. Of every ten couples who remarry, buoyed by love and renewed hope, six divorce yet again. *The eventual success of the new family hinges on the quality and strength of the stepcouple's relationship.* And the success of the stepcouple itself hinges on the willingness and ability of the partners to grapple with personal and family issues.

Few understand at the outset how complex and demanding stepcoupling is. Mary, remarried seven years, describes the early years of her stepfamily:

> *In the beginning, Bob and I and the four kids reeled from the effects of divorce. Looking back, the only reason we made it through the early part of our stepfamily was because we were such a strong couple. We had lots of problems. The kids fought all the time. My house was way too small for the six of us, and we couldn't afford a bigger one. A third of Bob's paycheck went to his ex-wife, so we barely made ends meet.*
>
> *Neither of us wanted another divorce. We had to learn how to talk to each other, love each other, and stay together even when things got tough. Especially when things got tough.*
>
> (MARY, THIRTY-FOUR, STEPCOUPLING FOR SEVEN YEARS)

Creating a stepfamily is like building a house. The stepcouple forms the foundation. If the relationship between partners is strong, the house makes it through the storms undamaged. If there are cracks in the foundation, the whole structure is in danger of collapsing.

Each member of a stepcouple must find ways to strengthen that foundation on a daily basis. Each must commit to the importance of "us" by setting aside time: for making love, sharing stories, solving conflict, laughing at private jokes, and dreaming about the future. Weekends away and other special occasions are grand, but they are not substitutes for daily connection. These simple moments will renew and strengthen the love that first drew you together.

A strong stepcouple also cultivates subtler habits that enhance their relationship.

When something significant happens in my life, Tom's the first person I tell. We talk on the phone at least once a day. He's my best friend.

(CARON, FORTY-TWO, STEPCOUPLING FOR FOUR YEARS)

I never leave the house without letting Nancy know where I'm going and when I'll be back. It's a small thing, but my first wife and I never did it.

(SCOTT, THIRTY-FOUR, STEPCOUPLING FOR TWO YEARS)

Larry gets irritated sometimes because I don't say "we" about things that involve the two of us. I try to remember to say "us" more.

(JANE, FORTY-ONE, STEPCOUPLING FOR ONE YEAR)

Why would a stepcouple need to be reminded to take care of their relationship? On an individual level, many adults who stepcouple don't know how to nurture relationships. Previous marriages may have atrophied from neglect. Depending on your childhood experiences, you may not even know relationships require and deserve care.

The very stresses that are unique to stepcouples—tight budgets, parenting obligations and conflicts, and ex-spouses—distract you from paying attention to each other and your relationship. However, if you postpone caring for your bond until other issues resolve, it may be beyond repair when you turn your attention to it.

Daily concerns, the ones you'd also face if you were single, still divorced, or in your original marriage, also compete for your time: the demands of children, careers, aging parents, and household responsibilities.

Regardless of stress, distraction, or lack of time, caring for stepcoupling *must* come first. Nurturing your relationship is the most effective way to ensure the health and longevity of your marriage and stepfamily.

Yet, by definition, stepcoupling never occurs in isolation. Successful stepcouples strike a balance among caring for their individual needs, their relationship, and the requirements of the whole family. Finding this equilibrium is particularly challenging in the early years. Just for now, though, shut the door on everyone else and concentrate on the two of you.

I've been divorced for nine months and just started dating. I know I'll eventually want to remarry when I find the right woman, but I'm not ever going through another divorce. The next one's for keeps. How do I get ready for a new relationship?

Successful stepcoupling begins with a successful divorce, which takes time. Preparing for a new relationship by regrouping and reconnecting with yourself is wise.

Two key emotional tasks occur during and after divorce: grieving the loss of a marriage, and renegotiating a new relationship with your ex-spouse. Until you complete these tasks, you remain emotionally tied to a past mate.

Divorced adults begin clearing a path to repartnering by taking inventory of a past marriage's negative and positive aspects. Certainly it's easy to describe what went wrong in a marriage just after a divorce. Strong feelings—of anger, hurt, rejection, failure—loom large.

These same feelings make it difficult to go through the equally important process of grieving the loss of a marriage's good qualities. By reflecting on the elements of your relationship that worked for you, as well as those that didn't, you free yourself to say good-bye and move on.

Former spouses then renegotiate their relationship, moving from the bond of a married couple to the courtesy, respect, and cooperation of coparents. Boundaries change as a once-tight connection becomes businesslike. Ideally, a shared commitment—to whatever is in the best interest of the children—continues.

Once the emotional tasks of ending a marriage are well under way, work still remains before you're ready for a new relationship. Sound advice comes in a hackneyed phrase: get to know and appreciate yourself. Explore your likes and dislikes, needs, goals, strengths and weaknesses, the patterns of your relationships, and your part in creating them.

Shelly, thirty-two, undertook this process deliberately. She sought therapy because her husband asked for a divorce. During their five years of marriage he'd had a handful of affairs, finally asking for his freedom. Despite resenting Nick's infidelity, she still loved him and grieved deeply over the end of their marriage.

Nick and Shelly completed the legal work for their divorce within a few months; her emotional healing took longer. Moving through denial and waves of grief and anger, Shelly rode the emotional roller coaster that follows divorce. Eventually she began to develop interests she couldn't share with Nick. She spent more time alone; he had thrived on an active social life. She sold the home they'd built and bought a vintage bungalow. Months later, she used her property settlement to start a small business; later still, she realized that she was happier without Nick than she'd been during the last years of their marriage.

As time passed, Shelly started dating. By the time she met the man she eventually married, she had honed her self-awareness and self-esteem. She knew she both wanted and deserved fidelity in a marriage.

Like Shelly's, your preferences, style, and usual responses are unique. Some elements of your personality are "hardwired"— part of your nature. Others are learned responses to your early environment (nurture).

Start the ongoing process of becoming better acquainted with yourself by considering the following questions. You could also ask a trusted and tactful friend to share his or her impressions of you.

- What makes you happy? What makes you sad? What makes you angry?
- What energizes you? What takes energy from you?
- How comfortable with change are you?
- How patient are you? Are you easily frustrated?
- What type of people are you drawn to? What type of people repel you?

- What kind of people do you attract?
- What type of people are you most at ease with?
- How wide are your mood swings?
- Do you feel strongly that things should be done in certain ways? Are you open to other people's ways of doing things?
- When you're troubled, how do you prefer to work things through: alone or with others?
- List five qualities you like about yourself—be honest.
- List five things you don't like about yourself—be honest.

As you develop a clearer picture of who you are—your temperament and personality—begin to consider how you interact with others. You learned a lot about relationships as a child, and you carry that information, consciously or unconsciously, into adulthood.

Here's a list of questions to consider as you contemplate the influence your childhood experiences may have on your relationships.

- As a child, did you feel loved, valued and respected?
- What was it like to be a boy in your family? What was it like to be a girl in your family?
- What was your role in your childhood home? Caretaker? Peacemaker? Scapegoat? Good child? Troublemaker? Clown? Baby?
- Who had the most power in your childhood home? Who had the least?

- How did your family handle disagreements? Did your family fight openly, discuss conflict or hide it? How did you handle your emotions as a child?
- What did you learn about money? What did you learn about sex? About the roles of men and women? About alcohol and other drugs? About relationships?
- What was your parents' marriage like? Intimate? Distant? Affectionate? Hostile? Mutually supportive?
- Did your parents stay married to each other or were there divorces and remarriages?
- Did you experience stepfamily life as a child?
- If so, did you get along with and respect your stepparent(s)? Did he or she respect you? What kind of relationship did you have? Affectionate? Hostile? Supportive? Competitive?
- Did you have stepsiblings? How did you get along with them?
- What were your parents like as parents? Loving? Controlling and authoritarian? Empathetic? Physically and emotionally available? Aloof? Permissive? Absent?
- How did you know you were in trouble as a child? How were you disciplined?

Some childhood experiences make it harder to develop and maintain healthy relationships. Conclusions you drew about life based on early experiences might include: men always leave, married couples fight, marriage isn't forever, don't talk about feelings, lies are OK if you get away with them. If you have concerns in areas like these, this is a good time to address them with the help of a counselor.

No matter what beliefs you developed as a child, they profoundly affect your adult relationships. Here are a few examples:

*After Fred divorced me, I was in mourning for our marriage, yet
I started dating. I was still attracted to men like him, ones who
teased me and put me down.*

*As a child, I'd done poorly in school and my family called
me "stupid." I acted "stupid." I was the butt of Fred's jokes,
too; I was used to it.*

*As I healed after my divorce, I outgrew acting dumb. My
new circle of friends didn't see me as dumb, either. It didn't feel
right to be around men—or anyone—who put me down.*

*When I met Bill, I was beginning to like myself. I knew I'd
be fine alone. I was raising my children and supporting myself.
He treated me like a competent woman, and I became more
competent. I can barely remember what it felt like to be in my
first marriage.*

*(SHARON, FIFTY-SIX, STEPCOUPLING
FOR TWENTY-EIGHT YEARS)*

Another voice on the same subject:

*My dad provided for my mom and the kids—new cars, country
club, nice vacations. My sisters married men who were good
providers. So did I the first time. We did the things young
couples on their way up do: big cars, big house, private schools.*

*The second time around I fell in love with a man who
doesn't have as much money. We have the world's greatest relationship—love, sex, family, laughter, and lots of fun.*

*For two years, we fought about how much money Rick
wasn't making. Until I got over my belief that men always provide for women, I couldn't fully enjoy our life.*

(JULIE, FORTY-ONE, STEPCOUPLING FOR FOUR YEARS)

Ideally, divorced adults become aware—of themselves and the influence of their history on their relationships—as they grow and venture out into the world of dating. In reality, though, many start new relationships before they know these issues even exist. Does that mean you missed the only opportunity to examine them?

Not at all. It's always important and never too late to revisit your past relationships, understand yourself better, and revise your beliefs and behavior as you tackle the challenges of stepcoupling. The sooner you begin this ongoing process, though, the better.

I've met the most wonderful man. We're incredibly happy together. My friends keep warning me that three months isn't long enough before deciding to get married. I can't imagine anything ever coming between us; why should we wait when it feels so good right now?

Love *is* fabulous. Nothing compares with the intoxication of falling head over heels in love. Surely no relationship in the history of mankind has ever been so wonderful, no sex so satisfying, no conversation so scintillating. Even the children seem charming. Expectations soar and problems wither in the blaze of new love.

Falling in love is even more wonderful if you're divorced or widowed because you're no longer alone. Everything you've always hoped for seems at hand. Intense, exciting feelings can sweep you into a remarriage and the creation of a stepfamily.

This, the honeymoon phase of stepcoupling, *is* magical. But like most magic, it's an illusion. Love's intoxication has a finite lifespan. After a period of ecstatic pleasure, normal life reasserts itself.

We went to a counselor right away. I hadn't been divorced long, and I wanted to make sure I wasn't falling into another unhealthy relationship. One of the first things the counselor told us was that we wouldn't always feel so in love.

I thought she was wrong, that we'd always melt when we looked at each other. She was right, of course. We still love each other very much, but the thrill of the first few months is gone. Our love is deeper now and we know each other much better.

(STEPMOM I, THIRTY-SEVEN, STEPCOUPLING
FOR THREE YEARS)

At some point early in a potential stepcouple relationship, engage your brain. You can still fall in love with the wrong person when you're thirty—or forty or fifty. By scrutinizing the quality of your relationships, you discriminate between the ones that merit a lifetime commitment and those that deserve a graceful exit before anyone, including the children, invests more time and emotional energy.

The questions to mull over in this early stage fall into three categories. If you respond honestly, you're likely to answer "no" to a question or two, indicating a likely area for eventual conflict. Several negative responses may point out a strife-riddled relationship.

1. **Is this relationship right for me?**
   - Does my partner respect me?
   - Does he or she listen to me?
   - Can I be honest? Can I show my real feelings and share my thoughts? Can I be me?
   - Can I rely on my partner?
   - Can I grow and change in this relationship?

- Am I able to reach my own goals within this relationship?
- Is my partner willing and able to help me?

2. **Does this relationship work for the two of us?**
   - Are both our needs being met?
   - Are we kind to each other?
   - Do I listen to my partner?
   - Do we include each other in our lives?
   - Can we be equal partners?
   - Do we have fun together? Do we share common interests and values?
   - How well do we resolve conflict together?
   - Are we both willing to compromise?
   - Are we friends? Can my partner count on me?
   - Is there room for my partner to grow and change?
   - Am I willing and able to help my partner?

3. **What's right for the children?**
   - Am I willing to be a stepparent? Is my partner?
   - Can I accept my partner's children?
   - Can my partner trust me with his or her children?
   - Can my partner accept my children?
   - Can I trust my partner with my children?
   - Can I respect my partner's relationship with his or her children?
   - Does he or she respect my relationship with my children?
   - Am I patient with his or her children? Do I honor them as individuals?

- Is my partner patient with my children? Does he or she honor them as individuals?
- Do we have similar parenting styles? If not, can we resolve our differences?
- Do we have similar expectations of our children?

In the early, infatuated phase of love, you'll be tempted to gloss over problems between the two of you. Don't. Particularly if you recognize a repeating pattern in your relationships, pay close attention. Some people can explore these issues on their own, others turn to friends for objective opinions. Still others need more structured guidance, either from a support group or a counselor.

When you're confident you're with the right person, savor this magical stretch of time.

Shortly after we got together, Chuck and I took the kids to the grocery store. As we went through the checkout line, we were joking and laughing. The checker said, "Your family looks so fun." I was thrilled! Not only was it the first time someone had called us a family, it was a such a contrast to my first family, in which we hardly ever laughed.

(VALERIE, THIRTY-SIX, STEPCOUPLING FOR TWO YEARS)

The early months of stepcoupling can feel marvelous. Enjoy them as much as possible and store up sweet memories to draw on later. Here's the rest of Valerie's story:

When we got home, I hurried to the phone and called a friend. Ten years or so ahead of me on the stepcoupling path, she said,

"Good for you! Remember every detail—you'll need it later, when things get tough."

A few months later, I knew what she meant.

When we first got married, we were able to talk about anything and everything. I know we're really busy with the kids and work now, but I feel like something's come between us. How do we get back to the closeness we used to have?

As the euphoria of early love wanes, uneasiness starts to emerge. The stepcouple begins to fear that something's amiss.

Little things start to bother you: your spouse's tone of voice with your child, for instance; how often he talks with his ex-wife; how he never picks up his dirty clothes. But perhaps you don't talk about what irks you, swallowing your complaints or dismissing them as petty. Annoyance festers.

Irritation over small issues reflects deeper tensions: unmet hopes and expectations, conflicting parenting styles, confusion, and anger. Consciously or unconsciously, you fear the strain in this relationship could mean another divorce. Many newly remarried parents distract themselves from this possibility with demanding careers, children, social activities, and/or travel. Emotional distance within the stepcouple begins to grow.

Around this time you begin to notice the children in the household acting out—either for the first time or more frequently and intensely. Their behavior creates additional stress.

As unspoken tensions mount within the stepcouple, you naturally begin to shift your attention from your relationship to your biological children. Once your marital relationship no longer feels so exciting or gratifying, you may wonder if you've made a mistake. You may even think you should have tried harder in a previous marriage. If you'd stayed, the children would have had more stability. "What have I done to my life?" you worry. "What have I done to my children?"

Feeling estranged from your partner at this point is part of the normal developmental process of stepcoupling, as is feeling guilty about your children. These feelings don't automatically signal your relationship's demise.

However, if your as-yet-untested stepcouple relationship is to endure, the two of you have to build a bridge between you. Find effective ways to connect with each other. Some strategies that work for other couples include phone calls and e-mail messages during the day, one night out alone during the week, dedicating time to talk together every day, and personal rituals of greeting and saying good-bye.

As a couple, you need to find your own way of connecting. If you're stumped about how to reach each other, reflect on the earlier, more relaxed moments of your relationship. When was the last time you felt close? What were you doing? Start with small steps and watch their effects.

Once the two of you begin to reconnect, even a little, take a moment to pay attention to what's working and tuck the knowledge away for future use.

> *Some friends took us to a concert. We were so stressed about our marriage that it didn't occur to us to do something fun together—we wouldn't have gone if they hadn't planned the evening and bought the tickets. As we sat there listening to the music, though, we held hands for the first time in at least a couple of weeks.*
>
> *On the way home, we agreed that we had to find more ways to relax together and have fun.*
>
> (*STEPMOM II, THIRTY-FIVE, STEPCOUPLING*
> *FOR TWO YEARS*)

As you focus on building comfort and trust in your stepcouple relationship, communication often becomes easier. In any event, communication is critical, because negative thoughts and feelings fester in silence. It's not easy for anyone to reach out in tense times.

> *My whole life I'd clammed up when things got tough. My first husband used to complain that I shut him out when I was upset.*
>
> *It was true. In my first marriage I gradually stopped talking because I was mad so much of the time. If something upset me, I didn't even think about bringing it up. Why bother? I figured.*
>
> *In this marriage I started out the same way, but I'd been down that road and knew that the only place it led was unhappiness and divorce. It helped that Rick didn't take my silent treatment personally.*
>
> *But it was* really *hard to change. I had to get to the point where I just couldn't stand clamming up anymore. I put both of us through a lot before I started talking about what bothered me.*
>
> *It's hard for me to describe just how bottled up I had to get before I started talking. If I'm really mad, I still sometimes shut up before I'll tell Rick why. But, overall, I deal with my feelings differently, by talking about them.*
>
> (JULIE, FORTY-ONE, STEPCOUPLING FOR FOUR YEARS)

When you're struggling in a stepcouple relationship, you may be tempted to blame your spouse for your difficulties. Blaming, instead of cooperating to find a solution, can destroy your marriage.

Blame destroyed Larry and Tamara's stepcouple relationship. Larry had dedicated himself to his son and daughter for the four years after his first wife left. He was a model father despite the number of hours his successful business required. He hadn't planned on dating before he met Tamara at a corporate gathering.

Intelligent and accomplished, Tamara initially found Larry's parental devotion charming. His highly nurturing parenting contrasted with her own father's distant style. She began to fantasize about having a child—something she'd never considered with another man.

However, Larry and Tamara never had a child together. After their wedding, Larry's devotion to his children continued at the same intense level he'd maintained before. Tamara didn't mind sharing Larry with his children during their courtship, but she became jealous of the time and attention he lavished on them after they were married. Increasingly angry, she felt left out and blamed Larry.

Defensive and angry himself, Larry blamed Tamara for changing her mind about what she wanted. He had been honest, he thought, about his children coming first.

As is the case with every conflict in a relationship, the truth lay somewhere between their two viewpoints. Remember, it takes two to tango and to tangle. Tamara was deeply wounded by her own father's indifference and had unconsciously expected Larry to nurture her emotionally. Larry, on the other hand, had decided to give without reservation only to his children, since a wife could (and did, in his first marriage) leave him.

Unfortunately, they never learned these truths about themselves or each other. Each wanted to blame and be angry more than they wanted to heal their relationship. After a few months of disappointment and hostility, they separated and divorced.

Here's an alternative to blaming:

Whenever we fought, Val would ask me what my goal was. Did I want to fix things between us, she'd ask, or did I want to be right? For a long time, I thought she was just provoking me. What a stupid question!

Later I understood why she asked. In my first marriage, my wife and I fought all the time. Whoever lasted longest won. Somebody always had to win, too, because we never compromised. Nothing ever got solved because we always fought over the same issues.

Early in this marriage I was fighting to win. I wanted to be right more than I wanted to have a good relationship. That's what happened: I got to be right, but I didn't feel close to Val. Now we fight less because she's taught me to look for what we agree about, instead of where we differ.

(CHUCK, THIRTY-NINE, STEPCOUPLING FOR TWO YEARS)

If your marriage is to last, now—in the tough times after the honeymoon phase—is the time to roll up your sleeves and start being honest with yourself and with each other. You have to sort through confusion, fear, anger, and disappointment to find the closeness you're looking for. Start with the topics that feel least risky, building trust that you're both safe enough to speak more honestly.

I feel like I'm losing my husband. It used to be so much fun to be together. Now it all feels like work. We argue, the kids need so much, and we never have any time together. Sometimes I just want to take my kids and run. *Help!*

It usually takes four to seven years for members of a step-family to feel like a traditional family—safe and comfortable.

Stepcouples have plenty of time to doubt their choices and capabilities in the interim.

As you start acknowledging and discussing the conflict in your relationship, you're likely to feel overwhelmed and confused. And for good reason. Your previous coping mechanisms—blissful denial of problems or stoic avoidance—no longer work.

Realistic, long-term solutions arise only when your issues and feelings are out in the open. With some basic communication skills and mutual determination to hang in there, you can begin to resolve conflicts one by one, chipping away at the wall of tension keeping you separate.

One of the reasons this stage of stepcoupling can feel so overwhelming is that conflict seems to emerge everywhere at once. A critical task for each member of a stepcouple at this point is to figure out how to juggle multiple demands.

Like it or not, when you repartner, you also step into relationships—close or more distant—with other people. At a minimum, you have new relationships with your stepchildren and your partner's ex-spouse. Often, the unfamiliar interactions include your partner's extended family, coworkers or colleagues, and old friends. The challenge that erupts now is dealing with new relationships, while at the same time figuring out how to be a partner in a new marriage.

When we married, I gained a stepson. I grew up with three sisters, I have two daughters myself. I didn't know how to have a boy around the house, much less stepmother one.

Jason took a ton of my mental energy at first. Whenever he did something that bugged me, I went through a whole mental process about how I should respond. First, I figured out if I was being unreasonable, then I figured out if I should cut him some slack because he's not my kid. Finally, I figured out if it was something I should talk to him about or if I ought to ask his dad to do it.

For example, he'd leave the toilet seat up and I'd clam up for two hours while I agonized over it.

Rick would ask what was wrong and I'd say, "Oh, nothing" because I didn't want to admit I was so upset over a stupid toilet seat. But I wouldn't be able to relax, either. Rick would wonder what he'd done. It was nuts, how much I let little things about Jason affect my relationship with Rick.

I had to talk to my friends with sons and to Rick to figure out what I could reasonably expect.

(JULIE, FORTY-ONE, STEPCOUPLING FOR TWO YEARS)

Not only do you acquire new relationships, your old ones change when you repartner. Your tie with your ex-spouse, for instance, undergoes some upheaval when you repartner. Your relationship with your children and with your own friends may also shift, now that you're no longer a single parent.

It would be wonderful to be able to define all the new and changing relationships one by one. Unfortunately, that's not the way life works in a stepcouple. During a single evening you may relate to your spouse, children, and stepchildren numerous times. Add a phone call or two and you might also step briefly into your roles as ex-spouse and new in-law.

As you become more comfortable with your role in each individual relationship, you can shift easily between them and, in fact, maintain them simultaneously. In the meantime, however, it takes mental and emotional energy. You may feel drained without knowing why.

The final factor contributing to your strain is that some of your relationships seem at odds with each other. Being a spouse can occasionally conflict with your role as a parent; taking the time to coparent with your ex-spouse can take time away from your current marriage. Some newly remarried parents report feeling that, no matter who they're spending time with, there's someone else who needs them at the same time.

How do you become more comfortable in all your new relationships? Time and trust contribute to your ease. The more experience and success you have acting in these roles, the more comfortable you are with them. Similarly, the more trust you have in the affection and respect of the people around you, the more comfortable you are interacting with them.

Throughout the process of defining new and changing relationships, you must remain clear about your loyalties. The positive energy for dealing with your confusion comes from your stepcouple relationship. When you feel loved and supported in your stepcouple, you face stepfamily challenges more easily.

Each partner experiences the sense of being overwhelmed. Each partner experiences confusion and conflict about the many new relationships. Each partner needs to rely on the pivotal stepcouple bond—one they might not yet fully understand—to get through this challenging period.

It's a paradox: the strain you feel comes from being in a stepcouple, and turning to your partner is the best way to deal with the strain you feel.

One of the moments when I felt my husband's love most was also when I needed it most. We were visiting his family—my first time—and I was sitting on the front porch talking to his brother. I'd been aware of how much of a stranger I felt, how much energy the weekend had taken. My husband walked out the front door, stood behind me, and reached down to touch my hair with a very tender gesture. It lasted two seconds, maybe, but it made all the difference in the world.

(STEPMOM II, THIRTY-FIVE, STEPCOUPLING

FOR TWO YEARS)

My husband is pressuring me to spend more time alone with him, but I don't think it's a good idea. We haven't been together long, but there's so much else to do—at work, around the house, and with the kids. I feel like we'd be better off spending more time taking care of things. We can romance each other when the kids are gone.

Nurturing your stepcouple relationship is the most important thing you can do for the long-term health and stability of your stepfamily. While special dates don't take the place of caring for your *us* on a daily basis, they can be wonderful.

Bill had sole custody of his two children; I had sole custody of my two. When we married, we were suddenly a full-time family of six. We were inundated.

Once a week, on Tuesday night, we'd go out. For us, Tuesdays were wonderful—we had each other all to ourselves with no interruptions. We'd sit next to each other in a booth, hold hands, talk nonstop. He'd talk about his day, I'd talk about mine. We'd plan for the future. We rarely talked about the kids. It was our *time.*

We knew the kids were safe at home. We also knew they were probably doing some things they shouldn't, like eating junk food or watching TV instead of doing homework. That one night, I could let go of control over the kids to have the time with Bill.

I don't think we would have become as strong a couple if we hadn't had our date night. Twenty-eight years later, we still go out once a week.

(SHARON, FIFTY-SIX, STEPCOUPLING
FOR TWENTY-EIGHT YEARS)

For many stepcouples, finances preclude weekly outings. Creativity can substitute for cash flow.

Sunday is a transition day for us. Once every two weeks or so, all our children go to their other parents' houses early on Sunday afternoon.

We wait a little while, to make sure that the kids aren't coming back because they've forgotten something, then we head upstairs. Our ritual is to make slow, sexy, Sunday afternoon love. We cuddle up for a long delicious nap afterward. Don't bother calling us on a Sunday!

We didn't set out to create that ritual, but we sure have grown to love it. We both know what we're going to do as soon as the kids leave.

(STEPMOM I, THIRTY-SEVEN, STEPCOUPLING
FOR THREE YEARS)

You might have to compromise to find a time-alone solution that works for both of you.

After my sons had been here for about ten days, Keith was ready to go out for the evening. I wasn't, because the boys were going back to their dad's soon. So we'd go out after they were in bed; my mom came over for an hour or so.

We didn't have time to do anything fancy, but we'd have a beer and a salad at a local pub. I couldn't have enjoyed myself if

I missed putting them to bed, and he would have resented it if we didn't go out at all.

(LINDA, THIRTY-SEVEN, STEPCOUPLING FOR EIGHT YEARS)

The time you spend alone is an investment. Each hour you devote to nurturing your stepcouple pays off many times over, both in the moment and later.

When we married, Rick had a cabin up in the hills. It's a long drive. Often, we go months between cabin trips.

Last month we had planned a trip, but we were both swamped with work. We'd already cut it back from three nights to one and were tempted to cancel it. All the kids were coming back for two solid weeks, though, the day after we were supposed to return.

We drove eight hours to spend twenty-four hours there. It was probably ridiculous, I suppose. But we talked all the way there and back and the peace at the cabin worked like it always does. I know that we dealt with the challenge of having all the kids better because we took that one day to go to the mountains.

(JULIE, FORTY-ONE, STEPCOUPLING FOR FOUR YEARS)

When my two stepchildren stay with us, my wife's completely preoccupied with them. The three of them don't include me in their activities. She says she loves me very much, and I love her, but I feel left out in my own home.

When you marry a parent, it's easy to feel like an outsider to your mate's relationship with his or her children.

Figure 1 shows the connections between members of a new stepfamily and explains why it's natural and normal to feel this way.

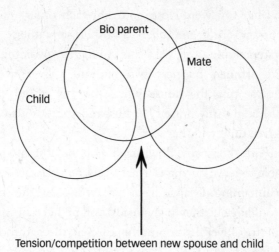

Tension/competition between new spouse and child

Figure 1. Competing Bonds in a New Stepfamily

Of all the connections in the fledgling stepfamily, the long-standing tie between parent and biological child is deepest. Even for a stepcouple with an intense emotional bond, the additional weight of biology in the parent-child bond means the stepparent is pushed to an outside position, at least initially. The arrow indicates the points of tension between stepchild and new spouse.

In response to feeling excluded, some mates resign them-selves to a part-time relationship, doing their own thing while their spouse spends time with his or her kids. Left unchecked, this tendency toward separation over the children can expand and undermine the stepcouple relationship.

Ed and Amy called a therapist because of ongoing conflict over Oliver, Amy's eight-year-old son from a previous mar-riage. Ed had also been married once before, but had no chil-dren of his own.

Amy shared joint custody with her ex-husband; Oliver spent half his time at his dad's house and half with Amy and Ed.

Amy and her son were close, enjoying each other's company, but the boy was rude and sullen toward his stepfather.

The stepcouple dealt with this conflict by avoiding it. Initially, Ed planned business trips around Oliver's visitation schedule, vacating the house when the boy stayed with his mom. Although Amy missed her husband, she was glad to have conflict-free time with her son.

Then Ed's company downsized, and he lost his job. No longer able to leave during Oliver's visits, he remained adamant about maintaining distance from his stepson. By the time this couple sought help, they had already assigned certain spaces in the house to Oliver: his room, the kitchen, the bathroom, and the family room. Any other rooms in the house were off limits. Oliver's hostility toward his stepfather increased, and Amy agonized over her desire to be loyal to both her son and her husband.

Ed and Amy proved unable to dissolve the camps they had established. Ed couldn't envision including Oliver in his household, much less his life. Amy didn't want to risk alienating her son by suggesting that the two of them include Ed in some of their activities. Ed and Amy divorced.

Figure 1, as well as illustrating why stepparents feel excluded, also depicts what needs to happen in a stepcouple where one adult's emotional tie with his or her children excludes the other. Over time, you must work to deepen the other two relationships: between the partners in a stepcouple, first and foremost, and between the new mate and his or her stepchildren. Figure 2 shows the results.

Nurture your stepcouple bond with your love, time, and attention, doing whatever fortifies it. Cultivate shared intimacies and a sense of humor. Develop private rituals before going to bed or making love. Use pet names for each other. Surprise each other with unexpected acts of kindness. As part of restoring your relationship, you also have to address the situation directly.

You'll always feel left out if you believe you have to compete with your stepchildren for their parent's attention.

My relationship with my stepdaughters is almost a barometer of my relationship with their dad. If I'm dreading their arrival, it's usually because I'm feeling insecure in my marriage. If I'm not feeling close to Chuck, I dread feeling pushed farther away when they get here. If Chuck and I are close and supportive, I'm OK with their visits.

(VALERIE, THIRTY-SIX, STEPCOUPLING FOR TWO YEARS)

If you feel as if you're competing for your spouse's attention, your stepchildren feel the same way. They'll stake their claim on your mate's attention and love more vigorously, exacerbating your feelings of insecurity. Competition begets competition—until somebody breaks the cycle.

Also, if you're insecure about your place in the family, your stepchildren are less likely to have faith that your presence will continue. They'll be less willing to include you.

Admitting to your spouse that you feel left out requires vulnerability. But openness and honesty can move the two of you closer and strengthen your relationship. You become more secure and less competitive. The children follow suit. In a noncompetitive stepfamily, there's plenty of room for all.

If you're the biological parent in a stepcouple, you're responsible for including your mate in your relationships with your children. Gently encourage your children to acknowledge and include your spouse. And if you're the stepparent, be flexible about the terms of your inclusion.

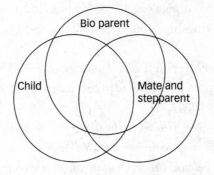

Figure 2. Emotional Bonds in a Healthy Stepfamily

Rick and his son go to movies—that's their together thing. One night they were going to a really stupid movie. Nothing I'd ever want to see. Just as they were leaving, Jason asked his dad if I wanted to come with them. I think he was too shy to ask me himself. You can bet I was in the car within a minute. I even bought the popcorn, I was so excited that Jason thought to include me.

(JULIE, FORTY-ONE, STEPCOUPLING FOR FOUR YEARS)

The other bond needing attention is the one between new mate and stepchildren. This relationship has to be developed, rather than strengthened, because it doesn't naturally exist at the outset of any stepfamily. One of the surprises of creating a relationship with your stepchildren is that it creates more room for and ultimately enriches your stepcouple bond.

Watching Scott teach Molly how to ride a bike, I was so grateful for him. I was grateful for all the work he'd put into creating a relationship with my daughter. I knew how hard it had been for him, how he'd feared her rejection. And watching him cheer

her on and the look of determination on her face, I felt a great
rush of love for him.

(NANCY, THIRTY-FOUR, STEPCOUPLING FOR TWO YEARS)

**After a few tough years, things finally feel more peaceful. We've
settled into a relationship and some routines that work for us—
and our kids. It feels so good. What do we need to watch out for
now that things are going pretty smoothly?**

The rewards of nurturing your stepcouple bond evidence
themselves on a daily basis now. You've become more adept at
dealing with stress, more comfortable and flexible in multiple
roles, more skilled at communication and compromise. You've
deepened your trust in each other and share a history that
enriches the present moment. You've come a long way.

The demands you face as a stepcouple, however, haven't
necessarily lessened. At any point along the way one of your
hot spots can flare. You can find yourself facing a sudden con-
flagration that feels all too familiar.

All the hard work we'd done seemed to fly out the window
when we faced the huge and unexpected expense of replacing
my stepson's car. I was furious when my husband caved in and
wrote a check without consulting me.

It was the worst fight we'd had in months. We barely spoke for
a couple of days. Then we remembered that we'd been in this place
before. That fight was about his son's needs versus our needs.

After calming down, I realized that Adam did need a car to
keep his job, and Ted needed to loan him the money.

It was a bad two days—and it was only two days. Earlier
in our marriage we'd have been afraid of getting divorced over a

*fight like this. Our emotions were intense, but we knew this
would pass and not separate us.*

*This was a blip—there'll be others. Thank God we can see
that they're blips now.*

(MARGARET, FORTY-SIX, STEPCOUPLING
FOR EIGHT YEARS)

As is the case with any couple, new problems and challenges can occur at any point. Illness, job loss, a troubled child,
and financial problems can threaten the equilibrium you've
worked so diligently to achieve. Some of the challenges, however, are unique to stepcouples; remarriage or redivorce of your
former spouses, changes in custody and financial agreements,
and birth of a new child are obvious examples.

We can all, regardless of our marital status, count on having
opportunities to grieve and rejoice, to fume and forgive, to let
go and love. In a stepcouple, you get more chances to experience the whole range of life's ups and downs.

And to share them with the one you love.

two

Tailoring Your Expectations
of Your Spouse and Family

Did you ever expect to form a stepfamily?

If you're like most people, in your youth you imagined an enduring first union. If you've never married, you probably imagine a typical first marriage, with only each other to care for. This is the picture our society paints and perpetuates.

When you do stepcouple, then, how do you know what to expect? Your perspective about stepfamilies also comes from popular culture, your history, and your imagination. Unfortunately, TV shows like "The Brady Bunch" misinform the public. No Brady stepchild ever said, "You're not my mother. You can't tell me what to do." No Brady stepparent ever felt like an outsider, and no conflict lasted longer than twenty minutes.

Your background—your previous marriage, if you've had one, and your childhood experiences—influence your expectations about stepfamily life. You naturally plug the past into your map of the future, without realizing you're doing it.

Our culture, too, embodies strong values about families—namely that happiness comes from a nuclear family. When Mom, Dad, and a small flock of loving, obedient children reside in a household, cheer finds a permanent home. If you fail to recognize this as a fable, you may believe that everyone who fits this mold has achieved domestic bliss. This paradigm, so ingrained in our culture as to be invisible, forms part of the standard against which you judge your new family. Evaluating a stepfamily by the standards you'd apply to a nuclear one is like grading an algebra exam with the key to a geometry final.

As a result—and whether you're aware of it or not—some of your initial expectations about yourself, your partner, your relationship, and your stepfamily are unrealistic. On the surface, your assumptions may sound reasonable. You're a mature, loving adult. You graduated from the school of hard knocks when you went through a divorce; if anyone's motivated to create a happy family, it's you.

You understand and love your children, so why shouldn't you understand and love your partner's children? Your spouse is bound to love and understand your darlings, too. By the way, you know what to expect from your children, and you expect his kids to behave the same way. It seems so logical.

Inevitably you'll notice a gap between your expectations and your experience. This gap is a source of the three Ds: disappointment, discord, and disillusionment.

Please note the distinction between unrealistic expectations and those that are appropriate in any relationship. You *can* expect that you and your children will be safe and that you'll be treated with respect in your relationship. If these basic expectations aren't met, you may have made a mistake in your choice of partner. However, you *can't* expect that your mate will anticipate and fulfill your every need, for instance, or cater to all of your children's caprices.

When you feel disappointed, you'll be tempted to point a finger at your partner or his or her children for letting you down. However, you need to learn to pause before placing blame.

For example, imagine it's the first holiday season that you're all together under one roof. Your previous holiday memories are warm and fuzzy. Now you have a new life with someone you love deeply. The two of you shopped carefully and planned surprises, and the gift-wrapped coziness you long for seems just around the corner.

Then you find your spouse in tears, grieving the absence of holiday rituals her first family shared. Your children fight during a holiday dinner. Your youngest stepchild cries himself to sleep three nights in a row.

Are you disappointed? You bet. Afraid that every year will bring the same emotional upheaval? Most likely. Angry and/or hurt? Definitely.

Stop and remember that disappointment, discord, and disillusionment signal the need for healthy adjustment in your stepcouple and stepfamily. Be patient with yourself and your family. Over time, as a healthy stepfamily matures, the gap between expectations and experience narrows. Everyone becomes more free to enjoy the unique experiences that stepfamily life offers.

I'm afraid that I've made a terrible mistake. I feel guilty that I don't love my stepchildren. I tell them I do, but I don't. What's wrong with me?

One of the best ways to set yourself up for failure in a stepfamily is by expecting too much from yourself. A pitfall of stepcoupling is to assume that love for your stepchildren follows—or should follow—love for your mate as naturally as summer follows spring. Ideally, over time, you develop a positive, healthy relationship with your stepchildren, but it may not include feelings of love.

You feel obligated to love your stepchildren for a number of reasons. All stepparents are initially uncertain about how they'll fit into their new children's lives. As a result, you may act like a television version of a stepparent: loving, kind, and patient in the extreme.

Some stepcouples, particularly those in which a biological parent has died or become inaccessible, yield to the temptation to leapfrog the stepparent into the role of loving parent. In still other stepcouples, loving each other's children is an implied condition of their relationship.

More generally, women feel pressure to conform to cultural expectations of being a good mother. Some women choose mothering as a proving ground in a new marriage. Both men and women may feel they have to perform for their spouses in the role of SSP—super stepparent.

You may also assume that your relationship with your stepchildren should be as close and loving as the one you have with your own children. While you may feel close to your stepchildren many years down the road, you'll always lack the biological parent-child bond that cannot be replicated. You won't share family history or the emotional and physical legacies that flow along bloodlines.

In reality, your relationship with your stepchildren grows over time, and no one can predict at the outset if it will eventually include feelings of love. Treat your stepparenting self more kindly by focusing on getting to know your new children as individuals, not worrying that you ought to feel differently about them. Instead of throwing a blanket of obligatory love over them, learn to understand them as people and appreciate their talents and other positive qualities.

> *My stepson of two years is thirteen. I still have yet to feel like—
> or tell him—I love him. I like lots of things about him, though.
> He's sweet and good-hearted and very, very funny. He kind of*

puffs up when I tell him how much I enjoy his sense of humor,
and I just love watching him try to come up with more jokes.

(STEPMOM II, THIRTY-FIVE, STEPCOUPLING

FOR TWO YEARS)

All of the above assumes that you simply don't feel as affectionate about your stepchildren as you think you should or expected you would. Painful disappointment and disillusionment can follow. Rather than being honest with yourself and your spouse, you may clam up and try harder to be an even more loving stepparent. This may only increase your disappointment as you exert more energy and only experience more disappointment.

If, however, you have negative feelings about your stepchildren and you're suppressing them, your stepcouple relationship is profoundly affected. Dislike or resentment of your stepchildren leaks into your relationship with your spouse in a variety of ways: you may become angry at your mate, withhold sex or emotional intimacy, or displace increasing anger onto your spouse's ex.

Alternatively, you may turn your negative responses inward, feeling a sense of failure as a stepparent. You may notice decreased energy or become depressed. You may adopt or increase avoidance behaviors, such as drinking or wanting to stay away from home more.

As unspoken conflict grows, your stepchildren—and your own children—act out more. Eventually, however, the cat claws its way out of the bag.

I thought it would be easy to love Bill's kids when we married.
I was so in love with him, how could I fail to love those kids? I
knew kids. Plus, I was a good mother to start with. The months
before we married were great.

Then I moved in.

As a full-time mom and stepmom my job was to help raise the kids. I had to set limits and discipline Bill's kids when he wasn't home. They hated it and acted out horribly. They missed their biological mom.

I took everything they said and did personally. All my lovey-dovey thoughts and high hopes flew out the window. I felt awful because I thought I was failing as a stepmother. Bill would come home from work, and I'd tell him what his kids did to make me mad. I begged him to do something about their behavior.

It takes a very strong person to listen to how difficult their children are. I really respect Bill because, even though I'm sure there were times he didn't look forward to coming home, he tried hard to keep anger from undermining our relationship. He didn't take it personally.

(SHARON, FIFTY-SIX, STEPCOUPLING
FOR TWENTY-EIGHT YEARS)

The first step in dealing with negative feelings is to become aware of them. Books and support groups, such as those offered by local chapters of the Stepfamily Association of America, a national organization providing information, education, support, and advocacy for stepfamilies, provide a forum for exploring feelings of all kinds.

You also need to discuss your feelings with your spouse as best you can. Unspoken issues fester, and partners distance themselves from each other. Risky as honesty sometimes seems, the alternative is worse: a relationship in which you can't be honest.

Use gentle communication skills and "I" statements to talk calmly about your feelings. Be open to your partner's feedback. Set a positive stage for future discussions.

Another important part of dealing with negative feelings toward your stepchildren is forgiveness. Absolve yourself for feeling the way you do. When you start talking to other stepparents, you'll be amazed at how common your feelings are.

Also, try to forgive your stepchildren for not loving you. Frankly, they didn't choose your presence in their lives. No matter how loving or indulgent you've tried to be, you most likely won't ever hold a candle to their biological parent.

Finally, hang in there and see what happens. Time is one of the best medicines for stepfamily ailments.

My first marriage had plenty of problems, but at least it felt like home. I love my current husband, and his kids are OK, but I can't call us a family. We're more like a bunch of strangers living in the same house.

The Stepfamily Association of America estimates that four to seven years pass before a stepfamily feels like a family to its members: safe, predictable, and comfortable. A strong stepcouple, aware of the issues involved in creating a stepfamily and willing to deal with them openly, can smooth the process.

Initially, you *are* a bunch of strangers living in the same house. You're missing the characteristics that define nuclear families: a common history, shared memories, family jokes, rituals, norms about appropriate behavior, even a shared surname. Early on in stepfamily life, the absence of these qualities stands in stark contrast to your previous family or to your ideas about family life.

This experience, although unsettling, provides a terrific opportunity for you and your partner to decide what your stepfamily will be like. Taking the perspective that you jointly create your new family over time, you remember that you're in

the middle of building something new to everyone. Gently
encourage the patterns you like and learn to take pleasure in
the process. You're not bound by old rules.

> *Early on, we dragged out the camera at every opportunity. I*
> *remember one night when the kids staged an impromptu per-*
> *formance. Keith got out his camera and took a whole roll of*
> *film.*
>
> *At the time, I couldn't have told you why we took so many*
> *pictures. Looking back, I can see that we were reinforcing our*
> *kids for being loose and goofy together. They still play like that*
> *from time to time.*
>
> *I got in the habit of putting the pictures in an album as*
> *soon as they were developed, something I'd never done before.*
> *But those kids pulled the album out all the time.*
>
> *It's like the photos helped them see how we were becoming*
> *a family.*
>
> (LINDA, THIRTY-SEVEN, STEPCOUPLING FOR EIGHT YEARS)

Encourage—rather than require—the behaviors you'd like
to see. Demanding that children act like family members when
that's not how they feel can lead to resentment.

You'll fare better by exhibiting a positive attitude toward
your stepfamily: its individual members, challenges, and novelty. Hold off on ponderous lectures about how you should
treat each other. Demonstrate inclusiveness, tolerance, and flexibility—and forgive yourself when you can't.

Model behaviors consistent with your notion of what a
stepfamily should be and watch your children's responses. You
probably have hopes and dreams for your new family, but your
children don't necessarily share them. As you gauge your chil-

dren's reaction to their stepfamily, you develop a better idea of how to proceed.

For instance, the language you use about your household conveys an important message to your children. Each stepcouple finds the vocabulary that works best. Some refer to themselves as a "family" from the beginning—this can work, particularly with younger kids. However, it can also backfire with older or resistant ones.

> *My dad's always talking about this big "family" vacation we're going on this summer. We're going to his wife's parents' house, even though she's not part of my family. My mom and my dad and my sister are my family. Everybody else is just part of the deal.*
>
> (RORY, TWELVE)

Here's another point of view on the subject of language:

> *We used the word* family *with each other, but not around the kids. Not until my oldest stepdaughter used it herself for the first time.*
>
> (RICK, FORTY-SIX, STEPCOUPLING FOR FOUR YEARS)

Children's responses evolve over time. Their initial reactions don't indicate long-term attitudes. As they get used to the new stepfamily, early positive and negative reactions can change dramatically, sometimes within a few weeks.

The challenges of stepfamily life are many, but the opportunity is unparalleled. Walk the walk, don't talk it. Go slowly, watch for distress signals, and take pleasure in small signs of stepfamily life as it takes shape.

In my first marriage, our family life was simple. Even though my wife and I had our share of problems, we were in charge. I don't feel the same way now. This is my home, but I'm not in control.

As adults, we all get one shot at a nuclear family. After the end of a marriage in which children were born, we never have a tidy, nuclear family experience again—no matter how much we want one or how hard we try to re-create it.

When visitation or joint physical custody is part of your children's lives, they're members of two different households. The large, diffuse family your children identify themselves as part of spans two or more households.

When my five-year-old draws a picture of her family, she includes different people. Her dad remarried recently, so his new wife hasn't appeared yet in her family pictures. There are usually two (her dad and me) or three (when she adds my husband) adults in her pictures. Her biological sister is always there and sometimes her stepbrother (my stepson). Her relationship with her new little stepsister at her dad's house is still pretty rocky, so she's shown up only once.

(JULIE, FORTY-ONE, STEPCOUPLING FOR FOUR YEARS)

Even though you don't live with the members of these other households, they impact your life in unexpected ways.

One Saturday evening, everyone sat down to dinner; it had been at least three weeks since we'd all eaten together. We were laughing about something, and Rick and I caught each other's eye. We cherish those magical family moments.

Not two minutes later, the phone rang. It was Jason's mom. Ordinarily, we wouldn't even answer the phone during dinner, but he was anxious to talk with her. The illusion that we were a regular family was broken.

I took that family feeling totally for granted in my first marriage. Now, even two minutes of feeling like a family is incredibly precious.

(JULIE, FORTY-ONE, STEPCOUPLING FOR FOUR YEARS)

You can't control what happens in your children's or step-children's other households, no matter how much you dislike the lifestyle or rules that apply there. As a stepcouple, you can jointly establish limits and standards that children adhere to in your home, regardless of how they behave in their other homes.

My stepdaughter's biological mom used to take her to PG-rated movies when I thought she was way too young. Lilly grew up much too savvy for my taste. We used to make sure she watched age-appropriate films with us, no matter what happened with her mother. You could say our efforts were futile, that we didn't protect her from anything. But in another way, it was an important statement for us to make about what was appropriate for young children in our family.

(LINDA, THIRTY-SEVEN, STEPCOUPLING FOR EIGHT YEARS)

Conflicts between households about standards and values are frustrating. Instead of becoming angry about what you can't control, however, focus on nurturing the family identity that the two of you want to create.

Early on, we set out to create some experiences that were special for our stepfamily. At the time, we had less money than either one of our ex-spouses, so we picked inexpensive things. Tent camping was a big success.

*Over time, we kept on camping. Our children's other par-
ents take them to Disney World and places like that. Part of
why we camp is still about money, but part of it's about something else. We want them to learn what's important to us:
peace, quiet, creativity, conversation. They don't get to sit
around a campfire with their other parents or climb into their
tent during a thunderstorm.*

*Camping is part of who we are. They're all asking if we're
going again this year.*

(MARY, THIRTY-FOUR, STEPCOUPLING FOR SEVEN YEARS)

Children can adapt to different standards in two different
homes. In fact, some evidence suggests that children benefit in
the long run. Their experience of different lifestyles and values
broadens the perspective from which they ultimately make
their own life choices.

**I don't know much about kids, because I don't have any of my
own. When I was little, children respected adults, period. My
stepchildren respect their father but not me. I certainly think I
deserve to be treated with respect.**

Stepparents and stepchildren alike deserve to be treated
with respect. While you should merit it simply by wearing a
wedding band, respect isn't natural or instant because of the
emotional upheaval in your new family. Respect emerges as
you get to know and adjust to each other and develop trust.

When there's open antagonism between members early in a
stepfamily's history, other issues lie under the tension. Unspoken anger, resentment, fear, grief, or other blocked emotions
often manifest as rude, rejecting behavior. It's unlikely that your

stepchildren will feel comfortable enough to communicate their negative feelings with you in a healthy way.

Any effort you make toward understanding what lies underneath your stepchildren's negative reactions will pay off. Step back for a moment and consider the situation from their perspective. They've lost their original family; why wouldn't they be angry?

My daughter Sarah seemed so two-faced. She'd act really pleasant around Valerie, but badmouth her behind her back. Val knew, and I felt like I was being pulled apart. One day I overheard Sarah griping to a friend again. I asked her to talk with me that evening. I told her that I wanted to know how she honestly felt about Val and that I could handle whatever her feelings were. I said I'd understand if she didn't like her, but that her behavior confused me.

Sarah started to cry. She said so much had changed in her life so quickly.

"I do like her," she said. "But I shouldn't like her. Mom's alone. It should be Mom with you."

(CHUCK, THIRTY-NINE, STEPCOUPLING FOR TWO YEARS)

When you're faced with rudeness and disrespect from stepchildren, it's tempting to draw yours versus mine battle lines: "She's your daughter. Can't you control her? My child wouldn't act that way." It's harder—and healthier—to deal with the issue as a stepcouple, discussing children's behaviors and feelings honestly and openly with each other.

Talk, too, about your own attitudes, expectations, and behavior. What language and courtesy do you demonstrate to the children in your stepfamily? How do you handle disagreements and misunderstandings? How do you want your partner to handle disagreements and conflict? Members of healthy step-couples and stepfamilies can disagree and still demonstrate a high level of respect for one another. Model the positive behaviors you'd like to see returned by your stepchildren. As hard as it may seem, don't take rude and rejecting behavior personally. It isn't about you, anyway.

> *Whenever Lloyd, my wife's ex, and I were in the same room, my teenaged stepdaughter was very rude to me. Her tone of voice, posture, and vocabulary made it clear that I was pond scum in her book. It never happened when she and I were alone.*
>
> *At first I was really hurt. I slowly realized, though, that it wasn't about me at all. By being rude to me, she showed her dad that he was the most important guy in the room. She showed him that no way was I going to replace him. Just understanding this made it easier to deal with.*
>
> (RICK, FORTY-SIX, STEPCOUPLING FOR FOUR YEARS)

If you don't feel respected by your stepchildren, examine your attitudes toward them.

> *When her dad and I first got married, my twelve-year-old step-daughter and I were like oil and water. Gina was so rude to me. I responded with insulting comments of my own. I hated her clothes, the friends she brought home, her activities, everything.*
>
> *This went on and on.*
>
> *One Sunday, an old family friend joined us for dinner. Later, she remarked on how my body language around Gina made my disdain for her clear. She told me she thought Gina*

was a delightful girl, vivacious and charming, and that I was clearly missing something.

I was stunned. But we'd been friends for years, and she wasn't a liar. So I had to look inside myself about Gina. For the first time I considered that her problem might be my problem, at least partially.

No magic happened. Gina still drove me crazy, but I began to consciously look for her strengths. Over time, I began to see them, too. I'd say our relationship really started when I realized that I might not be seeing her for who she was because of my own anger and hurt.

(SHARON, FIFTY-SIX, STEPCOUPLING
FOR TWENTY-EIGHT YEARS)

Feeling respected by your stepchildren takes on undue importance if you're insecure about yourself and your place in your stepfamily. If you don't have children of your own and marry someone who does, you're particularly vulnerable to uncertainty about whether you fit in and where.

So, once again, redirect your focus onto your stepcouple relationship, where it belongs. Ask your spouse to take you out for a cup of coffee or to dinner. Ask for whatever feels like love to you: the words "I love you," a long hug, a tender backrub. Ask to be reminded of what your spouse loves about you—and that he or she is committed to an enduring relationship. You married to become a spouse first and foremost. The more satisfaction and happiness you find in your stepcouple, the more tolerance and empathy you'll feel for your stepchildren.

Before our wedding, our children seemed excited about us getting married. When we were together, we had a good time and they

seemed to look forward to living in the same house. Since the wedding, though, it's not been easy or comfortable for anyone. What happened?

For stepcouples, fantasies and high expectations prevail before the wedding. You believe that your intoxicated feelings of love will last, and you're on your best behavior with each other and the children.

While some children resist stepcoupling from the beginning, others borrow your rose-colored glasses, initially seeing only the positive changes that a parent's engagement represents. A marriage may mean new playmates, confidants joining the family, or the reconstruction of a "normal" family.

> *"Oh good," said my youngest daughter when we told her we were getting married. "I love married moms!" Her reaction had nothing to do with Rick and Jason; she was just relieved I'd be married again.*
>
> (JULIE, FORTY-ONE, STEPCOUPLING FOR FOUR YEARS)

Your initial perception of a new marriage's reality is limited. A new marriage is like an iceberg; adults and children alike see the part that sparkles in the sun at first. Over time, you begin to sense the presence of a larger reality. The sunshine still glistens on the peak, but the dim bulk beneath the surface starts to draw your attention. You perceive the possibility of parenting conflicts, housing needs, financial constraints, personality differences and other issues.

Children often see and react to the darker side of a remarriage before you do. They hover on the edges of your love, rather than being consumed by it as you are. Wedding ceremonies carry symbolic weight for your children, as well as for you, and a wedding day can mark the transition between fantasy and reality. On that day, regardless of how long you've dated or been engaged, the deadbolt slides home in the door between your past life and the present. The sound is loudest for children.

> *I knew my parents weren't getting back together. But when the minister introduced my father and his new wife as "Mr. and Mrs.," I burst into tears. That's when I finally realized that it was over between my mother and father.*
>
> (RACHEL, FIFTEEN)

Some experts believe that the transition to remarriage is more stressful for children than the transition to divorce. During divorce, adults and children experience change and loss in unison. They undergo the upheaval of different housing, new employment, changed standards of living, new parental roles, new child roles, and additional household responsibilities together. Regardless of who pursued divorce, these events involve shared grief, loss, and change for adults *and* children.

When you stepcouple and create a new family, the adults view the accompanying changes as positive, healing events. Your gain, however, is your children's loss. They feel these losses—of parental time and attention, familiar routines, personal space—as deeply as you feel delight at having found someone to love again. Their grief, expressed verbally or behaviorally, is a normal response.

Seeing your children mourn while you're happy can be a profound disappointment. You may feel angry or impatient with them or fear that they'll never come to terms with your new marriage. Tolerating your children's negative emotions and responses can feel like an uphill battle.

Try to be open to their sadness and sense of loss and convey the message that all their feelings are welcome in this new home as everyone adjusts. As challenging as it can be, avoid taking their anger as a personal attack on you or your mate. Take comfort in the knowledge that time passing will help ameliorate their grief as they slowly adjust.

As you become aware of and sensitive to your children's experience of your remarriage, you may choose more private ways and settings to express your love for each other and joy in your relationship.

> *All three of our children used to hate it when we kissed. It wasn't anything torrid, either, just sweet little kisses as we passed each other in the kitchen. When we realized how they felt, we kissed less often when they were looking. We weren't letting them control us, just respecting their feelings about our displays of affection.*
>
> *(STEPMOM I, THIRTY-SEVEN, STEPCOUPLING*
> *FOR THREE YEARS)*

Finally, as a stepcouple, create an oasis for your relationship by doing whatever feeds your feelings of being a unified couple. By renewing your energy and sense of purpose as a stepfamily, you'll have more to give each other and your children.

Eventually, your stepfamily will feel happier and more comfortable as everyone adjusts. Hasten the day by allowing your children to be exactly where they are emotionally. As a stepcouple, recognize that anger and grief are part of building an enduring family.

I'm a much better father than my wife's first husband. He had an affair and left his wife and daughter; I spend more time with Amy

**than he ever did. I thought she'd be glad to have a good father. I
don't understand why she doesn't love and appreciate me.**

In stepfamilies, it's tempting to compete with your predecessors. This primitive, natural urge arises from the novelty of your situation and your insecurity in unfamiliar roles. You lack both a personal relationship with your stepchild and a clear idea of what it means to be a stepparent. You naturally fall back on trying to top the biological parent in terms of attentiveness, patience, playfulness, or generosity.

You can slip into the quicksand of competition before you're aware of it.

> *My husband's ex-wife sends the girls to us on weekends wearing rags, even though he writes her a big check every month. When they're here, I think it's important that they always have something nice to wear, even though it's sometimes a stretch for us financially. I take them shopping.*
>
> (STEPMOM IV, TWENTY-NINE, STEPCOUPLING
> FOR ONE AND A HALF YEARS)

> *My stepson complains that his mother doesn't pay attention to him, that she's too busy with work and her new husband. I think it's important for me to listen to him as long as he wants to talk. I'm very busy and not always all that interested, but I listen anyway.*
>
> (STEPMOM II, THIRTY-FIVE, STEPCOUPLING
> FOR TWO YEARS)

Rivalry always costs something: money, time, energy, or emotional reserves. You squander these resources when you compete with a biological parent, because you'll never win.

You can't win because you can't undo the past. Biology and history link parents and children in an intense and primal way, no matter how flawed you think the parent's personality or the parent-child relationship is. (In truth, the weaker your own relationship with a stepchild, the more critical you'll be of the biological parent.) You can't loosen or intrude on the biological parent-child tie—and you have no business trying.

Competition negatively affects everyone in your stepfamily. When you vie for king (or queen) of the hill, you're asking your spouse to negate the value of his or her relationship with a past mate. And competition puts your stepchild in the unfair position of choosing between adults.

You also lose yourself in the competition. Rivalry tempts you to overdo your natural inclinations. No matter how generous or patient you are, for instance, you succumb to the urge to be more giving or serene instead of responding honestly.

Often, resentment arising from going overboard is a clue that you're competing. A stepparent may think, "I took care of him when his mother wouldn't." Or, "I need a new shirt, but I have to buy my stepdaughter shoes because her father didn't."

Competing with your stepchild's biological parent takes the focus away from your stepcouple relationship. Remember, you remarried to become a spouse again, not a champion parent. As you shift attention to loving and being loved by your partner, your sense of security and purpose grows. Your need to compete with your partner's ex withers.

Relish the fact that you're happily married now. Let your spouse and his or her children have a past with another person. Your energy belongs in the present, not fighting a past that you can't change.

When you stop competing, you give your stepchildren three things they need more than the latest toy or treat. First, by focusing on nourishing your stepcouple, you model a healthy relationship between two loving adults. You increase the likelihood of the kids trusting this marriage, feeling safe, and learning how to make their own future relationships endure.

As you respond authentically to them, your stepchildren grow to trust you, because they're seeing the real you. Trust is the foundation for eventual respect and affection.

Finally, as you respond honestly and develop a healthy relationship with your stepchildren, you give them permission to do the same with you. Your example encourages them to develop a relationship with you that's based on more than what you do for or give to them.

three

Shaping and Knowing
Your Own Boundaries

A stranger standing too close for comfort. Intrusively loud passengers across an airplane aisle. Bear hugging acquaintances.

A coworker who sits alone at lunch. A standoffish business associate. A neighbor who just won't warm up.

Some people like to occupy your space; others wouldn't accept an engraved invitation to enter it. You're most comfortable when your unspoken rules about where "me" stops and "you" begins are in sync with the people around you. Your rules about what's "me" and "mine"—and what isn't—are *boundaries*. Your boundaries define your territory and you determine who can join you there.

Your sense of appropriate boundaries arises from your previous experiences: your family of origin and other relationships. There's nothing right or wrong about boundaries (with the obvious exception of abusive emotional or physical intrusion). Conflict arises when people have different needs for physical and emotional space and don't understand or accept those of another.

The examples that opened this chapter are universal, inconsequential experiences of boundary conflict. They last only a few moments. At most, you might experience fleeting anxiety or a flash of anger.

In a new stepfamily, however, boundary issues are common, persistent, and powerful. When a group of relative strangers moves in together, their differing emotional and physical zones can clash. Shared space and forced contact form a pressure cooker. Work or school can bring temporary relief, but the conflict waits at home.

Boundaries are particularly problematic in stepfamilies because they're different from first families. In a typical nuclear household, *family* includes all residents. Love them or hate them, they're your kin. In contrast, each member of a stepfamily has a different idea of what constitutes the family. Close biological ties extend beyond the threshold when children have a parent who lives elsewhere and/or when they go back and forth between households. Conversely, one member of a stepcouple may exclude the other's children from his or her emotional clan or a child may refuse to acknowledge a stepparent as a family member.

Boundary-related tension can arise between stepparents and children, present and former spouses, between members of the stepcouple, and among stepsiblings. Even within the ongoing relationship between biological parent and child, redrawing of behavioral and emotional lines occurs. Stepcouples must learn to recognize boundary conflicts and negotiate their successful resolution.

Conflicts over physical boundaries—what a closed door means, what areas are off limits to which members of the family, how common spaces are used—are obvious. Issues over emotional territory also occur frequently in stepfamilies. They present a greater challenge because of their more subtle and inherently personal nature.

For example, do you have emotional room for your stepchildren or is it too much of a stretch for you to include them? Do your children resent the energy you spend with your new spouse and his or her children? How comfortable are you encouraging your stepchildren to have a healthy relationship with their other biological parent?

Shaping boundaries is the process of establishing and maintaining emotional and physical space for individual members of the stepfamily, the stepcouple relationship, and the stepfamily as a whole. Healthy stepfamilies eventually develop consistent and sturdy boundaries that are sensitive to the complexities of their situation.

In the beginning, however, the absence of clearly defined physical and emotional spaces creates ambiguity and stress for everyone. Four factors contribute to the speed and ease with which you, as a stepcouple, can help your stepfamily resolve these issues.

First, you can recognize a boundary issue by the way it feels. Imagine walking into your bedroom to find your stepchild curled up on your side of the bed. How would you feel? Undisturbed? Anxious? Irritated? Infuriated? You can learn your characteristic emotional response to boundary violation.

Second, remember that conflict doesn't mean someone's in the wrong.

Adam used my towel to dry his hair before school. I moved towels and towel racks, everything I could think of to avoid picking up a damp towel when I got out of the shower. Finally, I exploded at him, "Would you want me to dry my hair on your towel?" He looked at me in a baffled way and said, "I wouldn't mind." It was a big deal to me and no deal at all to him.

(MARGARET, FORTY-SIX, STEPCOUPLING
FOR EIGHT YEARS)

Labeling needs for physical and emotional space as *right* or *wrong* shuts the door on successfully resolving the conflict.

Next, negotiating a solution depends on openly addressing the differences as soon as possible. Unspoken issues grow by leaps and bounds until you're incapable of considering someone else's position.

Last but not least, stepcouples must try to be flexible and inclusive. It eases their own path and also provides a model of adaptability for the children in the household. In a stepfamily, everyone must stretch their former comfort zones to include new people and unfamiliar ways of doing things.

You won't want to at first. Comfort zones are, well, comfy, and expanding them feels disquieting. But that's exactly what has to happen for a stepcouple and their stepfamily to succeed. Boundaries expand, and the loyalty that once flowed along blood lines loosens enough to permit a stepfamily to grow.

My seven-year-old stepdaughter invited her mother to her birthday party. My husband thinks it's fine if his ex comes, but I disagree. They're not married anymore, we are. I don't think she needs to be in my home for two hours.

You're right; she doesn't *need* to be in your home for two hours. Brainstorm alternatives. Perhaps you and your husband can move your stepdaughter's party to a neutral location, a restaurant or park. You could decide that you're willing to tolerate an uncomfortable situation for her sake. Would you be more comfortable moving the party to Mom's house altogether?

Many divorced adults duplicate special occasions and celebrations: two birthday parties and two holiday dinners. For many families who no longer live under one roof, this works fine. Graduation and wedding ceremonies can't be duplicated, however, so even previously married couples who haven't been in the same room for years must find a way to be together or decide who's going to be absent.

Other adults who are no longer married still celebrate together on occasions that are special to their children. Some are perfectly comfortable being in each other's homes for a few hours. Others may meet at a restaurant for a birthday dinner so that biological Mom and Dad can honor their children together. Still others can't tolerate being in the same space because of deep, still-unhealed wounds, so they shouldn't try.

There is no rule for deciding when to include—or exclude—the "other" parents. Every stepcouple has to come to an understanding of who's going to be part of the clan that gathers to celebrate. Developing and accepting this shared vision is part of the stepcoupling process.

Excluding the "other" biological parent is a natural impulse if you feel threatened and insecure. If you're part of a relatively new stepcouple, the bond between ex-spouses that is sustained by history and child-rearing can be intimidating.

When we were first married, Ted's ex-wife came over to talk with him and Adam, my stepson, about his grades. I didn't sit down at the table, but I could hear the conversation from the kitchen.

At one point, she used the phrase, "You know how your father is" to Adam. I had absolutely no idea what she meant.

I was the one who was married to him, but she knew so much more about him than I did. I felt this pit in my stomach, like we'd maybe made a mistake in getting married.

(MARGARET, FORTY-SIX, STEPCOUPLING
FOR EIGHT YEARS)

When you feel threatened by the presence of your spouse's ex, begin by consoling yourself with the obvious: You're the one with the license and the ring. Successful stepcouples eventually come to emotional terms with past partners. You can't delete your spouse's past liaisons any more than you can erase your own. Pay attention to the present and plan for the future with your spouse by strengthening your stepcouple.

Many stepparents also feel that allowing the biological parent into the stepfamily's territory threatens their relationship with their stepchild.

I'm embarrassed to admit that I'm jealous of the relationship between my stepdaughter and her mother. I think I should be bigger than that!

Emily and I get along great and have lots of fun when it's just the two of us, but when her mom comes into the picture, I fade into the background. She wants to show everything to her mom and sit in her mom's lap at the table—the same things she wants from me when her mom's not around.

I know I'm not the mother, but I'm particularly reminded of it when Emily's real mom is around.

(VALERIE, THIRTY-SIX, STEPCOUPLING FOR TWO YEARS)

Accepting that your partner has a former spouse and that your stepchildren have a biological parent takes time.

I was sitting in the parking lot at school, waiting for Lilly. Keith and I'd been together for just over two years, and it hit me suddenly that I'd never be Lilly's mother. She already had one, even if she spent more time with me. I felt a little sad, I guess, but I was also relieved to realize that I didn't have to compete for "Best Mom" anymore.

(LINDA, THIRTY-SEVEN, STEPCOUPLING FOR EIGHT YEARS)

As a stepcouple, once you've clarified the underlying issues, you can address what would most benefit the children in your family. Some children would enjoy having both biological parents at a special event. Many other children feel upset and torn when both biological parents are present.

The presence of both biological parents bothers children for several reasons. Older children often remember when their parents were married, and vividly recall the pain of separation and divorce. Seeing their parents together stimulates both sets of memories, and it hurts. Children who fantasize about a parental reunion may feel anxious or sad when they see their biological parents in the same room.

After our divorce, I was so proud that my ex-husband and I were civil enough to celebrate the girls' birthdays together. Rick eventually pointed out to me how uncomfortable Allison seemed when we were doing so. She wanted us to celebrate together, but she didn't know what to do with herself when we did. She was upset and confused.

(JULIE, FORTY-ONE, STEPCOUPLING FOR FOUR YEARS)

Work together as a stepcouple to decide who to include in family events. Take your individual feelings into account, as well as the feelings of the children. Be honest about what it will be like for everyone when the day comes.

If the two of you agree to include a biological parent, be proactive about taking care of your relationship. Make a plan for staying connected with each other. If you tend to feel threatened by your spouse's former partner, take preventive measures up front. Stay close to each other or check in from time to time. Offer and ask for extra assurance or attention in the form of a passing touch, a brief hug, or just eye contact. Talk to yourself, reassure yourself, stay calm and focused on the event. Remember why you're there. As best you can, ignore what the "other" parent is saying and doing.

Amicable former spouses can be tempted to use social situations to catch up on news about old friends and family. While this is a natural tendency, the spotlight belongs on the child when former spouses are together, so defer conversations like these to another time.

A final word on the subject: No decision is forever. When all the guests have gone, the stepcouple gets to sit down, put their feet up, talk together, and decide if they'll celebrate the same way next time.

My ex-husband calls me two or three times a day. He always has questions about the kids when they're here or about what to do when they're with him. I don't see it as a problem, but it really bothers my husband.

The flip side of excluding ex-spouses altogether is including them to a degree that feels excessive to a current partner. Other problematic boundaries include former spouses entering each other's homes at will and visitation that takes place on an "as needed" schedule, rather than being planned in advance.

Certainly, there are good reasons why you need to talk regularly with your children's other parent. Many biological coparents talk over large decisions—school issues, dating, driving, curfews, increases in privileges—together. However, these same parents handle day-to-day discipline and care decisions without input from a former spouse.

The reality is that your ex is no longer part of your residential parenting team. Depending on the age of your children, your present spouse should be gradually assuming the role of coparent with you and developing an ongoing relationship with your children. Too-frequent contact with an ex can interfere with your new spouse's opportunity to develop as a stepparent.

It's possible your ex keeps calling because he may not be able to relinquish control of your children's daily lives. He may be reluctant to relax his emotional tie to you or your children. He may not have moved on with his life. Divorced adults stay tied together for a myriad of reasons. Whatever the need your ex is attempting to address by calling, your responsibility is to shape an appropriate boundary, one that preserves and nurtures your stepcouple bond.

Also, consider why you're so willing to engage in frequent phone calls with a person you're no longer married to. Your ex can't intrude on your current relationship unless you allow it. A fuzzy boundary like this can represent unfinished work from your divorce. When you're not hanging up, you might be hanging on.

For the first few months, Scott and I talked about how often my ex-husband called me. The phone would ring at certain times of the day and we'd both know it was him. Sometimes I felt sorry for him and sometimes angry, but I kept answering.

One day, Scott asked me if Dave could please move out of our house. That's how it felt to him. He'd asked before but I'd never thought that there was anything I could do. It was Dave's problem—or so I thought.

I stopped answering the phone when I knew it was him. I'd check my voice mail and call back if it was something impor-

tant. It didn't take long before he stopped calling so much. I couldn't believe how much time and energy I'd spent talking to him while I was married to Scott.

(NANCY, THIRTY-FOUR, STEPCOUPLING FOR TWO YEARS)

Sometimes, understanding why it's been hard for you to set appropriate boundaries with a former spouse is enough to make the process easier. Guilt is another unresolved divorce issue that's often at work.

I get so furious when Ted won't say "no" to his ex-wife. If she wants him to drive Adam all the way up to her house and then pick him up again two days later, he does it. That's six hours of driving for a two-day visit.

I know it's because he still feels guilty that he's the one who ended the marriage. I hope he gets over it sometime soon.

(MARGARET, FORTY-SIX, STEPCOUPLING
FOR EIGHT YEARS)

Acknowledging the emotional reasons for your ongoing tie can go a long way toward building your relationship with your current spouse. Acknowledge, as well, the impact your bond with your ex has had on your present household. Be aware of the anger and jealousy that your spouse may feel.

If you're the biological parent, it's up to you to separate from your ex emotionally. By doing this, you create the coparenting space for your new partner to gradually move into. Begin to appreciate and affirm your partner's contributions to your children's lives, as well as his or her strengths as your resident coparent. Certainly, if you and your ex have shared all parenting, there's been no real need for your new spouse to take an active role, but he or she should feel involved. Seek ways to include him or her, if not in performing physical child care, then as an adviser or confidant when working through parenting issues.

The stronger your stepcouple relationship and the more time since your divorce, the less bearing your ex will have on daily events in your home, even if your children go back and forth between homes. Developing a unique and shared parenting style with your new partner can be a deeply gratifying reward of stepcoupling.

My husband's son is a pain in the neck. His room is a mess, even though I've told him that's not acceptable in this house. His attitude is awful; he never helps out and he's a horrible influence on my daughters. Sometimes, it's all I can do to be in the same house with him.

Accepting someone else's children, who are inevitably different from your own, and inviting them into your family is definitely a challenge. It takes courage, patience, tolerance, and maturity.

Unfortunately, many people, frustrated by their inability to control their stepchildren's behavior, exclude them emotionally. This reflex indicates serious stepfamily rifts. Ron and Claudia can tell you about it—but you'd have to ask them separately. They're no longer married.

Their short-lived stepfamily included Bob's fourteen-year-old son, Paul, and Claudia's daughters. Conflict simmered constantly between Claudia and Paul. Claudia disliked everything about her stepson: his clothes, taste in music, friends, table manners, food preferences. Paul ignored Claudia's initial "helpful" suggestions for change, and she became more demanding. Without being openly defiant, he dug in his heels, infuriating

Claudia. Her resentment became electric, and she bristled whenever her stepson entered the room.

The conflict expanded to include Ron when Claudia's initial comments to her husband about his son progressed to bitter complaints. Ron felt torn between siding with his son, who he believed wasn't doing anything wrong, and the wife he loved. Quiet and passive to begin with, he became more stressed and withdrew from Claudia. He felt guilty about the situation that he'd put Paul into and compensated for it by spending extra time with his son. Claudia felt unheard and unloved, viewing Ron's behavior as rejection and betrayal.

Claudia's anger and resentment began to splinter their marriage. The conflict escalated into a final "him or me" confrontation in which Claudia demanded that Ron send his son to live with his ex-wife. Ron refused, and their marriage ended after two rough years.

If you're living with a child who makes your blood boil, take the first small step toward dealing with the situation by considering the following questions:

1. Given that your stepchildren won't simply disappear, do you want your marriage to endure? If it continues, they'll be present. Is this prospect tolerable?

2. Are you willing to consider the possibility that you could have a different relationship with your stepchildren, even if they don't change?

3. Are you willing to consider including, rather than excluding, your stepchildren? Are *you* willing to consider doing something different?

Be as honest with yourself as you can. Stepcouples do break up over problems with children. One or more positive responses to the above questions means that desire and motivation to succeed can fuel you as you work through to a more comfortable state of affairs.

Begin by defusing the situation, focusing first on behaviors and feelings of your own that you can change immediately. Take a mental video recording of a typical negative reaction to your stepchild and play it back. What exactly are you doing? Yelling? Shaming? Losing control? If you'd rather see yourself in a different light, start by learning how to walk away and calm yourself down.

If you've been nagging incessantly, *stop*. Use brief notes or blackboard messages to make a request to a child who's been ignoring you. You still might not get a response, but you'll short-circuit a destructive pattern in your relationship.

Cease and desist constant blaming and complaining to your partner. It's not doing any good, anyway, and drives a wedge between the two of you. Consider finding someone else to vent to. If you can't afford a counselor or other professional listener, look for a support group in your area.

Once you decide to defuse the situation, realize that you have a serious issue with your stepchildren. Take a good look at why you find it so hard to expand your boundaries to include them.

If you haven't had much experience with raising children, you may be dismayed by the amount of patience and energy required. If you're feeling fragile and insecure about other areas of your life—your stepcouple, yourself, your career, for instance— you're probably unable to offer these resources to a stepchild. Moreover, you may feel as though the more energy your mate expends on his or her children, the less is available for you.

Alternatively, your commitment to guide and nurture a stepchild as a new stepparent won't be as deep as your commitment to do the same for your biological children. The biological tie is part of what sustains your relationship with your own children when they behave in unappealing, irritating, or destructive ways. If one parenting strategy doesn't succeed with your biological children, you're likely to pursue other options instead of throwing in the towel. Until your relationship with your stepchild deepens over time, you may be tempted to call it quits when they behave badly. Many stepparents feel this way sometimes.

If you're having trouble with a teenaged stepchild, you may not have much tolerance for adolescents. Teens can certainly challenge the parents who've known and loved them since birth, so your difficulty as a stepparent is understandable. Learning about normal development and behavior during this thorny period in a child's life can sometimes increase your understanding and patience. Many excellent titles on this subject are available at your local bookstore. Parents who've already navigated their children's teen years are another great resource.

Along similar lines, some adults who marry a mate with an adolescent child plan on just enduring the few years that remain until the teen leaves home. You may think it is possible to just grit your teeth and bear it:

> *My stepdaughter was fourteen when we married. I didn't like her very much, but I thought I'd wait the next four years out without being real with her. I'd be pleasant, but keep my real thoughts to myself.*
> (STEPDAD I, FORTY-EIGHT, STEPCOUPLING FOR SIX YEARS)

This strategy doesn't work. You suppress your thoughts and feelings at great cost to yourself and your potential relationship with your stepchild. You may eventually explode with backed-up feelings if you don't revise your strategy.

> *I realized I couldn't do it. It's so out of character for me to just be quiet when something irritates me. Also, I realized it wasn't fair to her. How would I feel if someone in my home was just waiting for me to leave?*
> (STEPDAD I, FORTY-EIGHT, STEPCOUPLING FOR SIX YEARS)

In addition to defusing the negative situation and exploring why it's so difficult, draw on the strengths of your stepcouple. Remember why you chose your partner and play on these pluses. Challenge yourself to find one positive characteristic about your stepchildren. If you're sincere, share it with your partner.

Finally, consider that you may have trouble with your stepchildren because you're competing with them for the lion's share of their parent's love and attention. So schedule some time with your mate away from the children and capitalize on it by enjoying your adult relationship. As you become more confident of your permanent place in your spouse's heart and home, you'll see that there's plenty of room for your stepchildren, too.

My wife and I have been married for two years, and we've been arguing because she says I'm closer to my daughters than I am to her. My girls and I became very tight after my first wife died, and my oldest will be leaving for college in a couple of years. I don't want to waste any of the little time we have left together.

A strong boundary that encloses the stepcouple is critical to the success of the entire stepfamily. To create the strong stepcouple relationship that supports and nurtures everyone in the household, adults must stake out physical and emotional territory that is uniquely theirs while continuing to meet the children's needs.

> *We taught our kids to respect our relationship. The respect we ask for is subtle, but it makes a difference.*
>
> *When we come home, we connect with each other before we do kid stuff. If we're talking with each other at home or in the car, we ask them to wait until we're done. They knock before coming into our bedroom.*
>
> (STEPMOM I, THIRTY-SEVEN, STEPCOUPLING
> FOR THREE YEARS)

Shaping this boundary sometimes means a departure from past patterns. When children and suddenly single adults deal with the death of a parent and partner, for instance, they often draw very close as they share deep grief and loss. While single-parenting after divorce or death, adults are often naturally tempted to turn children into adultlike partners and confidants during lonely times.

As parents repartner, tension emerges. Certainly, the tight parent-child relationship doesn't work for a new spouse who feels excluded. Balance is called for. The biological parent loosens the parent-child tie to create some emotional space for a new partner while remaining close enough to the child to meet his or her needs for comfort, guidance, and reassurance.

> *The Christmas after Chuck and I got married, we planned to travel to Kansas to spend the holidays with his parents. This is a family tradition for them.*

I remember how he dreaded telling his children because he knew what their reaction would be. They were very upset. The last two years, they'd gone to their grandparents' house with their dad, just the three of them.

When he told them, they said, "Why does she have to go?" And he said, "Because she's my wife and I want her to come with us." They were furious. For a while, things were pretty cold around the house. Chuck didn't give in and gradually they accepted the idea.

It was tough again right after we got there. But they got over being angry at us, and we ended up having a pretty nice time.

(VALERIE, THIRTY-SIX, STEPCOUPLING FOR TWO YEARS)

Strengthening the boundary around the stepcouple requires intention, time, and tact. It isn't always easy. Certainly, if your children have been very involved in your life, they'll resent an interruption to this pattern.

You don't have to push your children away, however, to make room for the two of you. Gently hold the line around your stepcouple. Acknowledge to your children that things are different now that you've repartnered. Acknowledge their feelings. Statements like "I know you're angry that we're not doing this alone" allow you to connect emotionally with your child and still preserve your stepcouple bond. Assure your children that you love them and you love your spouse, too.

While the process of drawing the boundary around your stepcouple can be challenging, the rewards are worth it. A healthy, well-developed stepcouple relationship is intensely gratifying for adults.

There are also huge rewards for the children in your household, although they may not be consciously aware of them. A healthy adult relationship provides the emotional foundation for children to flourish and grow. Children experience genuine caring and concern between adults as deeply reassuring.

> *If you ask her, Emily will tell you that she'd like her mother and me to remarry. But you should see the look on her face when Val and I are tender with each other. I don't mean in a sexual way, because she never sees that.*
>
> *But when we hug or rub each other's shoulders, any of the ways we say "I love you" during the day, her face sometimes shines. She's loyal to her mother, but I think she's glad that my marriage is strong.*
>
> (CHUCK, THIRTY-NINE, STEPCOUPLING FOR TWO YEARS)

A strong stepcouple relationship allows your children to grow and attend to their own urgent developmental needs. When your emotional needs are being met in a healthy way by your stepcouple relationship, your children are more free to move fully into their own futures.

My own children and I have always been physically close—lots of hugging and cuddling. This closeness doesn't feel right in front of my stepchildren because I'm not comfortable treating them the same way.

When you stepcouple, you're called to examine behaviors and activities that felt perfectly natural before. Suddenly, spontaneously hugging your own child can leave a stepchild feeling left out and lonely. Because it's so easy for a stepfamily to fragment into insiders and outsiders, you must figure out how to help everyone feel like an insider. Children thrive when this fundamental need—to know they belong—is met.

When my daughter Beth and I watch movies, we lie down and cuddle on the couch together. I'm glad she still likes to do that, even though she's in high school.

When Jason's in the room, though, it feels awkward. I wonder if it bothers him. I think it does because he seems restless.

(JULIE, FORTY-ONE, STEPCOUPLING FOR FOUR YEARS)

Some stepparents try to treat everyone the same. If they hug their kids, they scoop their stepkids up, too. But because everyone has a different comfort level with physical affection, it's a better idea to consider how your hugs might be received and proceed more slowly.

One alternative is to take your cue from the style that your partner has with his children. If his affection toward them comes in the form of pats on the head, a bear hug from you can feel like an invasion. Later on, maybe they'll appreciate your style, but they'll probably find you overwhelming or intrusive in the beginning.

Another way adults in a stepcouple try to treat everyone the same is by giving their own children what they're comfortable giving their stepchildren. If they don't hug their stepchild after a weekend away, they don't hug their own children, either. This well-intentioned effort to equalize affection bewilders biological children and is ultimately painful to parents and children alike.

When we all moved in together and I was suddenly the only mother, it was overwhelming. In addition to the fact that my mother self had to spread out over more children, I also felt like I had to treat all the kids the same. So I sort of backed off from my own children physically.

> *If there's one thing I could go back and change about those*
> *years together, I'd give my own children more hugs and not*
> *worry so much about being fair.*
>
> (SHARON, FIFTY-SIX, STEPCOUPLING
> FOR TWENTY-EIGHT YEARS)

Another awkward situation arises when one parent is very physical with his or her children. Maybe your new partner found a way of connecting with your children, but you aren't comfortable getting close to hers. Maybe being overly physical wasn't the way you were raised, or the way you treat your own children. Maybe your relationship with your stepchild is too new, and you just don't feel close enough yet. Despite any internal or external pressure you might feel to become physical, honor your discomfort. If you're uncomfortable, your stepchildren will be, too.

Developing a different approach for each child in your household is okay, as long as your overall goal is to connect somehow with everyone. All children's needs and likes are different, anyway. Obviously, how you connect with your stepchildren will vary with their ages and genders. A seven-year-old is likely to be more receptive to a hug—and more approachable—than a seventeen-year-old. Men might understandably be more reluctant to get physically close to a stepdaughter, women to a stepson, especially as they get older.

This reluctance can arise from being aware of the possibility of sexual energy between unfamiliar adolescents and adults in close quarters. Although this can be more of an issue when a new mate and a stepchild of the opposite gender are close in age, racing adolescent hormones don't discriminate well. Being sensitive to all potential effects of physical contact on your stepchildren helps you fine-tune your behavior.

Remember, physical touch is just one way of expressing affection and caring. Listening, spending time, keeping agreements, praising or appreciating, and honoring them as individuals are all ways of connecting with your stepchildren. Even a simple gesture like maintaining eye contact while your stepchild speaks goes a long way toward conveying the fact that you care and are there for them.

Physical play is yet another avenue for making contact.

We play a lot in our house. My daughter Allison hangs on Rick's arm while he tries to lift her feet off the ground. Beth and I try to tickle each other. Jason and his dad wrestle, and I occasionally steal Jason's hat and try to keep it away from him or we arm wrestle. Everybody needs some physical contact, and play is a pretty safe way to do it.

Over time, I've watched Allison begin to turn to Rick. She'll crawl into his lap or lean up against him. Just the other day, Beth leaned on him while we were all in the kitchen. That was the first time she approached him for some contact.

(JULIE, FORTY-ONE, STEPCOUPLING FOR FOUR YEARS)

Over time, you'll develop a way of expressing affection that works for you and your stepchildren even if it is not the way their biological parents do so.

Jason and his dad are very physical with each other. From the time I first met them, Rick would give Jason back rubs or rub his shoulders.

We've been together for a while and I still don't relate to my stepson the same way his dad does. I'm really "huggy" with my own children, but I mostly give him little pats on the back or shoulders. I'm still working on finding ways to connect with him.

(JULIE, FORTY-ONE, STEPCOUPLING FOR FOUR YEARS)

As you develop as a stepfamily, expressing affection comfortably through words and gestures gradually becomes second nature.

My stepson hates me. For three years I've done everything I can, but he still resents me like crazy. If anybody calls me his stepdad, he tells them that I'm not any part of his family.

It is very difficult for some children to accept that a first family is over. The older the child, the more resistance he or she is likely to have to a newcomer in the role of a parent's partner. Older children are more loyal to their biological parents, so divorce and remarriage are more disruptive. Also, the developmental task of teens is to move away from the family unit. Integrating a new person into the family runs counter to this imperative.

Many children feel angry at their biological parents when they repartner. It often feels too risky to express that anger toward their parent, so they displace it onto the stepparent. The greatest challenge you face when cut out of your stepchild's definition of family is to avoid taking the rejection personally. This is, by the way, much easier said than done.

Eight months after we married, my stepdaughter turned thirteen. Before her birthday, our stepfamily was discussing how to celebrate.

"I know what I want," Gina said. She turned to her dad and said, "How about if our family goes out for dinner?" Bill said fine, and asked me what I thought.

"No, Dad," she said. "I mean just us." She pointed at him and her brother. "Just our family, not them."

I felt like I'd been punched in the stomach. Gina meant that my sons and I weren't invited on her birthday because we didn't fit inside her definition of family. I felt like an outcast.

(SHARON, FIFTY-SIX, STEPCOUPLING
FOR TWENTY-EIGHT YEARS)

Constant rejection by a stepchild can be a huge test of your stepcouple relationship. Your challenge is to avoid getting angry back.

I felt shocked and hurt, and Bill felt pulled apart. It took hours of talking for us to understand the situation and reach a solution we both could live with. We decided to share a family party the night of her birthday, and he took her out for pizza the next night.

(SHARON, FIFTY-SIX, STEPCOUPLING
FOR TWENTY-EIGHT YEARS)

It's tempting to rail against a rejecting stepchild and demand that your spouse do something about the behavior. This tactic doesn't work. You may see some brief, superficial improvements in behavior, but the child's anger and resentment increase underneath the surface.

Don't deal with a rejecting stepchild by asking your partner to collude against the child, agreeing that his or her behavior is unprovoked and intolerable. In essence, the biological parent abandons the child to his or her anger. When this happens, the child becomes an unvalued outsider in the home and is deeply wounded. Behavior problems escalate as the child becomes less and less able to connect with the biological parent.

Do recognize that you're dealing with a child's unresolved and unspoken issues. Distress, not malice, prompts children to declare "Get away from me!" Assume that a rejecting stepchild is so overwhelmed with feelings of grief, loss, and anger that he or she must lash out. This understanding can help you avoid taking it personally and, more important, begin to understand your stepchild's experience from his or her point of view.

Try telling the story of your household and your stepchild's life from his or her perspective. If you find this difficult, try completing the following phrases:

My stepchild is sad because _____ .
He or she is grieving the loss of _____ .
One reason he or she is so angry is because _____ .
What my stepchild will remember about this time in his or her life is _____

_____ .

What we can do to help him or her with the anger and loss is _____

_____ .

Consider asking your partner to tell you about his or her child. Be curious, rather than angry. Listen more than you talk. The healthier your stepcouple relationship, the easier it is to cope with challenges. Turn toward your partner to meet them, not away.

When things were rough between his daughter and me, my husband and I tried to be a couple whenever we could. When

*we went away on weekends, we tried to let ourselves leave the
tension behind, emotionally and mentally. Almost always, we'd
eventually remember something to laugh about.*

*This worked so well. Not only did we break the tension,
but when we went back, we could remember what we'd found
funny, at least for a while. It was like recharging batteries.*

(LINDA, THIRTY-SEVEN, STEPCOUPLING
FOR EIGHT YEARS)

Scheduling time alone between biological parent and child
is also important. In all likelihood, a stepchild who is rejecting
the stepparent feels profoundly threatened by the new adult
relationship. Special time with Mom or Dad reassures the child
of his or her importance. Keeping to the agreed-upon time is
critical. A broken promise confirms a child's worst fear and is
worse, in this situation, than a promise never made.

Scheduling this time, rather than waiting for a spontaneous
opportunity, lets the child know that she's as important as
everything else on your calendar. A stepparent who actively
supports the time a parent and child spend alone together sends
a powerful message of acceptance and value.

A child who is acting out anger and loss is unable or
unwilling to express his or her feelings. A calm biological parent can give permission for a child to talk.

*I was seeing a counselor when Beth was going through the
worst of her anger at Rick. The counselor said that I needed to
give Beth permission to express anger in front of me, not just
act it out. I already felt so guilty about the changes I was making in her life that it was really hard for me to listen to her tell
me how she felt about the changes.*

The counselor told me I had to keep my mouth shut and listen. And I have to say that things started improving between us when I started listening.

(JULIE, FORTY-ONE, STEPCOUPLING FOR FOUR YEARS)

The biological parent should try to get out of the middle of an angry relationship between stepchild and stepparent. The biological parent can work toward encouraging both child and partner to take their concerns to each other. This honesty is very challenging in the beginning.

I remember the first time I said, "Please talk to her, not me" while my wife, Val, was griping about Sarah. For way too long, I had listened, feeling like it was my job to do something to make things better between the two of them. I felt like the weight of the world had been lifted from my shoulders when I stepped out of the middle of their mess. As long as I let her complain to me, she didn't have to do anything to make their relationship better.

(CHUCK, THIRTY-NINE, STEPCOUPLING FOR TWO YEARS)

Hang in there. Put yourself in your stepchild's shoes. Nurture your stepcouple relationship, and wait for the tincture of time to take effect.

We've been together under one roof for two years. My stepson, who used to visit every other weekend, just moved in. It was a good move for Shane, but my oldest daughter is being so difficult. She won't leave him alone when he's on the phone, and she criticizes him constantly.

Children who visit every other weekend remain partially outside the stepfamily boundary. Their sporadic presence provides a pressure valve for stepfamily issues. When a visiting child moves in for good, a stepsibling may try to keep the former visitor in an outside position.

Particularly in relatively new stepfamilies, the status quo already feels fragile to children, and a stepsibling moving in seems to threaten the balance. The attempt to close ranks is defensive, and not a deliberate act of spite. On the other hand, the entering stepchild has to establish a position within the stepfamily. To make this transition easier for everyone, the stepcouple must strike a balance between creating physical and emotional space for the child moving in and letting stepsiblings work things out for themselves.

Adults are in charge of setting guidelines that make clear there's room for everyone within the family. Together they consider what has to change now that all the children live in one home most of the time. Will common areas be used differently? Who uses which bathroom at what time? Do bedrooms need to be switched? How can privacy be maintained? If possible, would moving to a new house altogether give everyone a fresh start? Providing solutions proactively can avert some conflicts over space.

Children already living in the home also have different routines from those who stay only a few days a month. Some parents don't bother assigning household responsibilities during weekend visits. It's also tempting to delay assigning them until a child has settled in. However, equal distribution of chores means that everyone's on a par, so the sooner this happens the better.

For the child moving in, household responsibilities convey, in no uncertain terms, that they're an important part of family workings. For the children making room for a newcomer, sharing household tasks with the newcomer means that the special privileges that often go along with being a visitor are over.

Trying to make sure that rules about respect and responsibility apply to everyone is a step toward making sure everyone's an insider. However, children who have trouble adjusting to the new configuration of a stepfamily may resist the rules intended to support it. You may have to work overtime to get them to stick.

> *No matter what the situation, my oldest stepdaughter is always trying to get the upper hand. We make the rules—like nobody eats in the family room—and then find that she's broken them. It's her dirty dish on the couch—again. We have to follow up with her four or five times more than with anyone else. For some reason, she thinks the rules apply to everyone but her.*
> (RICK, FORTY-SIX, STEPCOUPLING FOR FOUR YEARS)

What exactly are the rules? That's up to the two of you. One of the most rewarding parts about being in a stepcouple is taking advantage of your past parenting and family successes to create the family experience you want.

As your stepcouple becomes stable and the two of you decide on the rules you're going to rely on, consider implementing them within a family meeting. In this way everyone has a chance to share concerns and opinions. The stepcouple welcomes everyone's input, but the adults ultimately set the policies and rules. Family meetings look like a democracy, but they're more like a benevolent dictatorship. The stepcouple's in charge.

In addition to creating behavioral guidelines that make clear that the family boundary includes everyone, the stepcouple also has to allow the children to work some things out on their own.

Before Jason moved in, he and Beth got along great. She'd invite him to movies or to go to the mall.

Man, did things change when he moved in. All of a sudden, she didn't like anything about him. They went for a long time without speaking to each other except when they had to.

It was really hard to let them be. The one thing I did was to refuse to let either one of them complain to me about the other. I did it more for me than them, but it forced them to deal directly with their own feelings.

(JULIE, FORTY-ONE, STEPCOUPLING FOR FOUR YEARS)

When a stepcouple sets the tone of inclusiveness in a household, children eventually follow suit. The message that adults must repeatedly convey, gently and firmly, is the truth about successful stepfamilies: *Everyone is at home here.*

My wife thinks all the kids should take turns doing the dishes. My son already takes out the garbage and cuts the grass, which are harder chores than those the other kids do, so I don't think he should have to do dishes, too. We just can't agree.

In a stepfamily, it sometimes seems like your own children get the short end of the stick too often. The impulse to protect them is entirely natural, born of loyalty and instinct.

It's also dangerous. Biological protectionism creates the potential for separating into two mini-families in the same household. When this happens, a stepfamily breaks along bloodlines, and although they continue to share a home, two smaller, biologically defined families draw rigid emotional boundaries around themselves. Each remains fiercely loyal to their own.

When this happens, adults may base children's privileges on kinship rather than age, responsibility level, or unique needs.

Sometimes the money in one mini-family stays there, with little exchange across the boundary. Occasionally the two mini-families eat meals at different times or even take separate vacations. These variations seem to make perfect sense to the adults involved, but they reflect deep conflict within a stepcouple.

Every stepfamily feels some "us" versus "them" tension. How much is too much? One troubling sign is regularly protecting your children from the other members of your stepfamily because you're anxious or angry about the way they're treated. Your stepfamily may also be starting to split along bloodlines if you constantly resent your spouse for championing his or her children's causes. If you're talking to your children—or to yourself—about what's wrong with "them," you're on shaky ground. You might need help to erase the chalk lines that you're drawing down the middle of the house.

Successful stepcouples recognize the pull to separate along biological lines and take steps to reduce it. They find a way to help everyone balance genetic allegiance with loyalty to the larger, more inclusive stepfamily. They both acknowledge differences and work toward defining an "us" that outweighs them. These stepcouples realize the possibilities that arise out of negotiation and compromise.

My stepdaughter wears heavy boots. After she moved in, the wear and tear on the floors was hard, so I asked her to take her boots off at the door.

It seemed like a simple request, but her dad resented it. He thought it wasn't fair because her boots were harder to get on and off than anyone else's shoes. I thought that didn't make a difference because she could choose to wear something else.

In the end, we decided together that the only thing we could do was to ask everyone to take off their shoes in the house. It's a

> *pain for all of us, but it is fair. And it works; the floors don't get*
> *so dirty.*
> (LINDA, THIRTY-SEVEN, STEPCOUPLING FOR EIGHT YEARS)

Another strategy for counteracting the tendency to form two mini-families is cross-pollination. In a garden, bees cross-pollinate flowers by transferring the pollen from one species to the stamen of another; rich surprises result. As a stepcouple, look for opportunities to get to know and support each other's children.

> *We decided that I'd help Sarah register for her freshman classes.*
> *My oldest niece had already been through the process, and*
> *I knew how it worked. I enjoyed helping her figure out what*
> *to take.*
> (VALERIE, THIRTY-SIX, STEPCOUPLING FOR TWO YEARS)

Supporting or appreciating your stepchild in front of your own children dramatically conveys the message that you're all part of the same stepfamily.

> *One of the riskiest things I ever did—and the best for our step-*
> *family—was to call my seventeen-year-old on her rudeness to*
> *her younger stepbrother in front of everyone. She was surprised*
> *and furious! But she got the message that, as far as I was con-*
> *cerned, her behavior wasn't acceptable family behavior.*
> (JULIE, FORTY-ONE, STEPCOUPLING FOR FOUR YEARS)

Feeling like your children get the short end of the stick in your stepfamily? They do. So do your stepchildren. That's because many stepfamily sticks have two short ends. It's just harder to see the end your stepchild's holding.

I have to remind myself that her girls don't get everything their way, either. I'm tempted to think that my son and I are on the bottom of the heap, but when I stop and really look at what's going on, it usually is relatively fair. We work hard at making it fair.

(RICK, FORTY-SIX, STEPCOUPLING FOR FOUR YEARS)

Time together gradually reduces the pull of biological lines as trust and communication grow. Until it's no longer an issue, though, it's up to the stepcouple to make sure that their home holds only one family that includes everyone.

My husband's ex-wife is a vindictive snake. She doesn't pay child support even though she's supposed to and has way more money than we do. She changes visitation or cancels it at the last minute. My husband and I both hate her and there's nothing we can do to get her out of our life.

Nothing suffocates stepfamily fantasies faster than a hostile ex-spouse.

I married Ted thinking that I'd finally have the family I wanted. I couldn't have kids of my own, so I'd love his. Life would be good.

Marcia, his ex, ended that in a hurry. She resents me and does everything in her power to screw up our time together—not just family time, but also chances that Ted and I have to get away. This isn't at all what I thought it would be.

(MARGARET, FORTY-SIX, STEPCOUPLING FOR EIGHT YEARS)

Chronic rage between ex-spouses is a catastrophic and tragically frequent outcome of divorce. While adults do suffer from an acrimonious divorce, the real tragedy plays out within the hearts of the children involved.

From a child's viewpoint, *family* is defined by biology, not marital status. When divorced parents struggle to push each other out of the boundary around the first family, they sabotage the emotional health of the children. A stepparent joining the fray magnifies the emotional devastation.

Children are driven to love their parents. When a stepcouple conveys, subtly or explicitly, that a biological parent is unlovable and unworthy, a child experiences internal conflict. He or she questions and/or suppresses natural feelings of affection and loyalty. At a minimum, voicing anything positive about the offending parent becomes out of the question.

Whether your ex or your spouse's wears a black cape, you'll be sorely tempted to rail against the villain. Don't do it. Scream into a pillow, write letters that you never mail, go to church, seek therapy, play tennis really hard. Do anything to deal with your anger and resentment *except* vent or display it within earshot of your stepchildren or children. That includes body language and facial expressions.

Rage also costs a stepcouple dearly, independent of its devastating effects on children. Of course, you and your new mate will be tempted to create a cabal of anger. When you're angry, you naturally want to spew and be validated. How many times in your life have you felt understood and vindicated when someone agreed that they, too, would be furious if they were in your position?

Here's the catch. Anger is seductive and self-perpetuating—and an utter dead end for you. You can be furious from now until kingdom come, and it won't make one bit of difference. All the vocabulary, time, and energy you put into anger at the ex is being diverted from other, more important areas of your life.

Whenever I'm tempted to get mad at my ex, I remember a guy I met once. He was so mad at his ex that he'd spent thousands and thousands of dollars trying to get his kids away from her. He couldn't afford a house, so he lived in a cheap apartment. His legal battles took up so much time that he quit his job to try to screw her. He was totally possessed by rage.

He didn't have the kids. And he didn't have the kind of life that would have provided much for his kids even if he had them.

(STEPDAD I, FORTY-EIGHT, STEPCOUPLING
FOR SIX YEARS)

Here's the ultimate irony about what happens when a stepcouple colludes in anger toward an ex-spouse: The ex gets exactly what he or she wants. Ex-spouses who seem to sabotage your relationship want a loud and clear presence in your home. When you talk constantly about what a jerk your ex-husband is or plot ways to foil his ex-wife, you grant that presence. Maybe the ex isn't there physically, but he or she rules your life emotionally.

Successful stepcouples take care of the children in their home—and themselves. They find a way to honor the boundary encircling the first family, acknowledging the presence and value of both biological parents in a child's life as much as possible. They avoid maligning the absent parent at all costs, even when sorely tempted.

Her dad is a twit. I think he's worthless and unreliable. But half of her comes from him; I just keep remembering that. If I talked about what a creep he is, I'd be talking about part of her. I can't do that.

*Plus, there are some good qualities about him. I mean, what
does it say about me if I can only see the bad in the man I
picked to have children with?*

(STEPMOM *III,* THIRTY-THREE, STEPCOUPLING
FOR ONE YEAR)

Take some comfort from the knowledge that yours is an
age-old predicament. Remember how King Solomon arbi-
trated a dispute between two women, each of whom claimed
an infant was hers? His advice? Cut the baby in two and give
half to each. The first woman begged the king to spare the baby
and give it to her rival. The second agreed that half a baby was
better than nothing at all. Solomon judged the first woman to
be the infant's real mother.

Make use of your power to choose: spare the baby.

Allow the children to have a relationship with their parent.
As they grow, they may discover on their own the good and
not-so-good parts of the parent.

*When the boys got older, they could see that their dad was
nuts. I never said anything to them—and, God, was it hard—
but they started making little comments about how weird and
self-absorbed he is.*

(STEPMOM *V,* FORTY-THREE, STEPCOUPLING
FOR ELEVEN YEARS)

As a stepcouple, support each other in maintaining appropriate boundaries. Learn how to say "no" when appropriate—
and use the right criteria to gauge appropriateness.

*The girls' dad constantly changes visitation at the last minute.
He's so important and busy that he can't keep a commitment.*

It's unbelievably frustrating, because I can't depend on any arrangement until the very last minute.

Sometimes I want to refuse his requests, just to set a limit. Rick always reminds me to think of what the girls would want and not act out of my own frustration. They can handle all the changes much better than I can.

(*JULIE, FORTY-ONE, STEPCOUPLING FOR FOUR YEARS*)

Remind each other in words and gestures that you're married to each other now, no matter how infuriating a past partner is. Tell your new partner: "You're right, she might be awful. But let's don't spend our time together talking about her. I want to be with you." Set a firm emotional boundary that keeps a sabotaging ex from infiltrating your personal space.

Refusing chronic rage spares the baby and saves the stepcouple. This is simple to say, but hard to do—and no stepcouple task is more important.

four

Rewriting Roles—A Feat of Family Acrobatics

Imagine starting a new job. You've changed careers, so you have no experience. To make things worse, you don't understand your new job description; you have no idea what your responsibilities really are. As you interact with others on the job, you realize you don't know how to respond or behave.

Welcome to stepfamily life. Few stepparents—or stepchildren or stepsiblings—have any experience with their new roles. What you think your job description is arises from your past experiences—your first family or your childhood—and it doesn't map well onto this new position. In fact, clinging to the wrong job description means it will take that much longer before you're comfortable in your new role.

To compound the issue, no universal job description exists for any stepfamily member. Every new stepfamily shapes these roles, over time, in a way that works best for them. How you, and the other members of your stepfamily, write your roles depends on several factors.

First, as mentioned above, your own history heavily influences what you believe your role should be. Any childhood experiences with or in a stepfamily will shape how you interact in one as an adult. If your background is in a traditional nuclear family, you'll spend some time sorting out the differences between the adult roles in a first family and those in a stepfamily.

The other half of your stepcouple also influences the way you play out your role as partner and parent. In an ideal world, members of a stepcouple have similar visions of how they'll function as parents and stepparents. More often, partners have to work out the differences in their behaviors and expectations before reaching a mutually satisfying agreement. One partner may want a spouse to move instantly and completely into the role of parent—a daunting prospect for many new stepparents.

How the two of you interact will also affect your role. Do you collaborate on parenting issues or maintain independent camps? Do you discuss or fight about differences or tend to sweep them under the rug? Around your house, is the style "every man for himself," "one for all and all for one," or a blend of the two?

Similarly, how you interact with your stepchildren helps determine how your job as a stepparent evolves. Do you sit around the dinner table and talk over the day, or do the children in your stepfamily bolt the moment they swallow their last bite? Do you favor a familiar or more formal style toward them? Do you engage with the friends they bring home? Are you an active stepparent or do others provide the lion's share of parenting and nurturing?

Your stepchildren's residential or visitation schedule also influences how your role develops. If they only visit every other weekend, the part you play in their lives will be different than if you share a house all or most of the time.

The ages of your stepchildren will impact your role in their life—and theirs in yours. A preschooler makes room in his or her life for another influential adult far more readily than an adolescent does.

Clearly, it takes time and perseverance to develop and refine your new job description. Willingness is required, too: to get to know the people in your new family, to sort out the various forces impacting all of you, and to get to know what you're comfortable with. During the process, rely on what works for you and what seems to work for the people around you. Eventually, your new role will feel natural and reflect the unique style of your stepfamily.

And, lest you think your role can be carved into stone, remember this: The only constant in stepfamily life is change. Get as comfortable as you can with who you are in your new stepfamily—and be ready to change with circumstances.

I expect my wife's kids to follow my rules and to answer to me if they don't. My wife thinks I should take it easy since they're not used to having me around. I think she's too soft on them.

The fundamental question involved is whether or not your new role as a stepparent includes disciplining your mate's children. Let's look at what motivates children to behave in accordance with rules.

In healthy parent-child relationships, the rules are reasonable, rational, and consistent. Everyone understands them, and the child knows that the cost of going against the rules is a temporary loss of approval and trust from his or her parents. Parental authority derives partially from a child's need to feel trusted and approved, and the emotional validation for behaving appropriately is enormous. In short, children naturally want to please their parents.

New stepparents sometimes assume that their role comes with immediate authority as a parent. They believe they should be obeyed by virtue of their position in the stepfamily. Sometimes, assuming that you have *positional authority* works with a young child, particularly in the honeymoon phase of step-coupling.

> *When Nancy and her three-year-old daughter moved in, it was obvious that no one had disciplined Molly for a long time. She was out of control and didn't mind anyone. She didn't know what "no" meant. She terrorized the house. I decided that I would set boundaries with her, even if no one else did. I know how to be firm. She spent a lot of time in time outs, and things got a little better.*
>
> (SCOTT, THIRTY-FOUR, STEPCOUPLING FOR TWO YEARS)

The tragedy when too much discipline comes too early is what happens to the relationship between stepparent and stepchild. Here's the next part of Scott's story:

> *I was Mr. Discipline for about four months. Then Molly began telling me that she hated me. She'd have nothing to do with me, and she'd cling to her mother. It was clear that what I was doing wasn't working.*

Scott realized that he needed to change his behavior if he was going to have a relationship with his stepdaughter. Her willingness to engage with him increased as he interacted with her for purposes other than changing her behavior: to play a game, read stories, or go for walks. Finally, he realized that everyone would be served best if his wife remained the primary disciplinarian; he could support her as his wife learned to set effective limits.

An older child, particularly a teen, is more likely to oppose a stepparent's early efforts at discipline, blatantly challenging or silently ignoring requests and rules. You may be tempted to up the ante at this point, cranking up consequences in an attempt to force compliance. Doing so creates a no-win situation for everyone: a power struggle.

> *My stepson moved out of the house he shared with his mother and her new husband, Al, because Al insisted that Michael obey him without question. Michael refused because Al wasn't his father, and they reached an impasse. Al couldn't or wouldn't back down, and Michael just wouldn't accept him in a parental role. Michael's behavior got more and more out of line. They yelled at each other, slammed doors, and things seemed to be escalating. Finally, the only recourse was to move him here.*
>
> (STEPMOM II, THIRTY-FIVE, STEPCOUPLING
> FOR TWO YEARS)

A successful stepparent focuses on developing a relationship with a stepchild, generating *personal authority* in the process. As you—and your trust and respect—become personally important to your stepchild, he or she will become amenable to your requests about behavior. It just takes time to grow this relationship.

Cultivate trust and respect by getting to know your stepchildren as individuals. Learn their likes and dislikes, interests and strengths. Affirm their accomplishments in the world and allow them to get to know you.

> *Lilly and I were lucky that our relationship developed so slowly. Her dad and I dated for a couple of years before we got married, and she and I got to know each other's pet peeves and foibles pretty well. When Keith and I got married, some things*

*came up but I basically trusted that she was a good kid. She
trusted that I cared about her. I'm glad I didn't become a stepmother any sooner than I did. I wouldn't have been ready.*
(LINDA, THIRTY-SEVEN, STEPCOUPLING FOR EIGHT YEARS)

Cultivating a relationship with your stepchild is more than
becoming a best pal. Balance being a friend with maintaining
an adult role. Many stepparents have compared the position to
that of a benevolent aunt or uncle—an adult first; a friend,
advocate, and mentor second.

While building a relationship with your stepchildren, nurture your stepcouple by supporting your partner, behind the
scenes, in parenting his or her children. Offer suggestions if he
or she wants them. Listen with a sympathetic ear to the challenges of parenting in a stepfamily and applaud your partner's
successes.

Stay somewhat detached. These aren't your personal parenting struggles. Remember why you got married in the first
place. It wasn't so you could shape up his or her kids.

In some stepfamilies, career demands mean that the biological parent is often absent, leaving the stepparent in charge.
These families face the challenge of making sure children
behave without creating resentment for the stepparent when
the biological parent is away.

One strategy is for the stepcouple and child to go over
ground rules together. The biological parent appoints the stepparent as acting authority in his or her absence. The biological
parent makes it clear that the child is to obey the stepparent. As
a stepparent, your main responsibility is to remind the child
about the ground rules, enforce them, and let your partner
know how things are going.

I was really nervous the first time my husband went out of town. I'd never been alone with his son before. We went over the rules, and I planned ahead in my mind how I would deal with him when he got out of line.

In reality, we did just fine. We cooperated to get things done around the house.

(STEPMOM II, THIRTY-FIVE, STEPCOUPLING

FOR TWO YEARS)

When you're faced with misbehavior, you can remind your stepchild that you realize you're not the parent. However, the parent did ask you to follow through on the house rules, and you intend to do your job. You are the adult in charge, after all.

Handling parental absences in this way—or a similar way that works for your stepfamily—keeps your role clear. You can focus on building trust and goodwill, the keys to the authority you earn.

I always wanted to be a mother, but I can't have children. I thought that by marrying a man with a daughter, I could be happy. It isn't working for me. I can't stand doing the things I think a mother would do, because she isn't my child.

Stepmothers with no children of their own often plunge into what they believe the role of a mother should be. However, raising someone else's children can't replace the experience of having your own offspring. When you realize this, feelings of grief and loss about not having your own children can overwhelm you and make it difficult to function as a stepmother.

Certain behaviors and feelings trigger your disillusionment. First, children inevitably misbehave, fail to appreciate adult efforts, are demanding, get mouthy, make messes, and generally act like children. Becoming aware of your stepchildren's imperfections is often the first crack in the fantasy of perfect motherhood. ·

Second, let's face facts: Caring for someone else's child is inherently different from caring for your own flesh and blood. Other people's children bother us in ways that our own don't. Your child's dirty feet and ragged toenails reflect a healthy, active life; your stepchild's dirty feet might be utterly repulsive. Your child chewing gum with an open mouth is a bad habit; your stepchild chewing with his mouth open can be maddening. Not to mention dirty underwear, grimy socks, and body odor. The physical proximity of living in a stepfamily means that you're privy to the personal habits of small and not-so-small strangers.

Finding your stepchildren to be fleetingly distasteful is a universal experience. And while we ordinarily advise open communication within a stepcouple, this is one instance where you'll want to find someone else to vent to. Even the most grounded and confident parent finds it hard to avoid taking offense when a mate spouts off about how disagreeable his or her child is. Complaining about characteristics a parent can't change about his or her child will only serve as a wedge between you and your partner—and there's nothing wrong with the child in the first place.

Instead of complaining, look carefully at your assumptions about your job description. Begin with a list of the specific activities you resent doing on behalf of your stepchild. By focusing on individual behaviors, you can discriminate between the ones that really rub you wrong and those you can tolerate. Also list any activities you genuinely enjoy.

Second, consider each activity carefully. Does your stepchild really *need* it? Some are necessary; many others reflect your misconceptions about what your role ought to include.

Leaving emotional needs aside for the moment, all kids require meals, clothes, hygiene, a safe and nurturing environment, transportation, and occasional help with homework.

Examples of optional activities may include getting your hair done together, cleaning rooms, whipping up gourmet treats, elaborate shopping trips, movie nights, trips to baseball games. Eliminate the unnecessary care you resent providing.

> *I'm not a morning person, but after Bill and I married, I tried to be the perfect cheerful mom in the kitchen every morning because I thought I should. I am not cheerful in the morning. After about six months, I gave up. It was easier for the kids to get their own cereal. I set the boxes and bowls out on the counter before I went to bed. I made sure they had enough food, but I didn't serve it.*
>
> *I felt slightly guilty, but they didn't need me nagging them about the time or telling them I didn't like their outfits.*
>
> (SHARON, FIFTY-SIX, STEPCOUPLING
> FOR TWENTY-EIGHT YEARS)

Consider, too, whether you're the only one who can or should provide the things on your list. If there's an activity that you just can't stand and it also happens to be very important to your stepchild, can someone else take it over? An older sibling? Your spouse? Their other biological parent? Grandparent?

Ideally, you'll end up with a realistic, feasible list of what your stepchild requires from you and what you can commit to providing. These are the elements of your evolving job description. Odds are it'll be much shorter than what you started out with. Reconceptualize your role in your stepchild's life based on the list you now have. Also look to your stepcouple for help in reframing your job in the family.

When I married Bill, I took on the job of helping him raise his children. That's the way I think about it. They have a mother; I'm not their mother. I'm a partner and coparent to their dad, and I do what will help him and his children.

(SHARON, FIFTY-SIX, STEPCOUPLING FOR TWENTY-EIGHT YEARS)

Resentment will arise if you forgo all your own needs to take care of your stepchild. If this is true for you, be sure to resume activities that nurture you. Chief among them is your relationship with your partner.

Recently, I went through a period of really resenting Jason for the mess he makes around here. No matter what room I entered, it seemed like I'd find a trail: bread crumbs, dirt, water on the bathroom floor. It seemed like a major part of my job as a stepmother was to clean up after him. I felt like a slave.

I felt really resentful. Then I realized that since Rick had changed his schedule, he'd been gone most evenings. Not only was I solo parenting more, but I also wasn't getting enough time with my husband.

Once I realized what I was really angry about, I talked with Rick. We arranged for some alone time, and he paid more attention to me when he was home. He did a little more work, too.

I stopped being so angry at Jason.

(JULIE, FORTY-ONE, STEPCOUPLING FOR FOUR YEARS)

The process described here—moving from resentment to rewriting—takes time, from months to years. Revising roles also happens more than once, as circumstances and needs change over time. As is the case with many stepfamily issues, flexibility is key.

When my stepkids visit every other weekend, I get anxious and angry before they get here. I hate it when my husband expects me to be the nice, accommodating stepmother. I love him, and his kids are good kids. What's the matter with me?

You're ahead of the game by realizing that you get upset anticipating your stepchildren's visits. Many adults become tense a few days beforehand. They find fault with their spouses or withdraw from them. They get too busy to engage with the arriving children, become ill, or distract themselves in other ways. Unfortunately, too few recognize the pattern or understand why it happens.

Your discomfort has three sources. First, you're a stepparent by default. You chose to become part of a couple; the fact that it's a stepcouple was beyond your control. Your mate came with children, and so you have no choice about assuming the role of stepparent to some degree. Understandably, you resist taking on that role.

Visiting stepchildren also disrupt the pattern and flow of your stepcouple relationship. It can feel as though their presence and legitimate needs upset the well-ordered and relatively private life you and your mate enjoy. You resist the interruption in your routines.

However, you must accept and learn to fulfill the responsibility to your stepchildren that you took on when you married your mate. Acknowledge your resistance, understand why you feel the way you do, and gently turn your attention to finding ways to reconcile your roles as stepparent and spouse.

In the beginning, when both roles are new, this is hard to do. It's particularly challenging to switch between roles.

When his kids come, I feel like I have to store up, in terms of Chuck's affection and attention, for a few days beforehand. Then I sort of bid him good-bye until they go. It's like "See you on the other side."

Obviously, we still see each other while they're here. But our relationship feels different. I'm not as comfortable being openly affectionate with him in front of his children, and I'm stressed trying to figure out how to be with them, too.

Basically, I don't think I'm doing a very good job as either a mate or a stepparent right now.

(VALERIE, THIRTY-SIX, STEPCOUPLING
FOR TWO YEARS)

Time will help. The more experience you have at filling two roles at the same time, the easier it becomes. Also, successful stepcouples intentionally look for ways to stay connected when they're focusing on parental roles. Quick, tender gestures make a difference; so do inside jokes and moments alone. As your confidence in your stepcouple grows, you can afford to be less possessive.

On the other side of the equation, growing into your own version of a stepparent takes time, effort, and sacrifice on your part. If your spouse's view of your role differs from your own mental job description, the process is more difficult.

Often, a biological dad wants his new wife to fill the functional shoes of a previous spouse. Society supports this notion. Women should be caretakers, warm and available to children. If you don't fit the mold, you can feel like a failure.

It's even worse when your stepchildren are good kids. You think: "I should feel differently. What's the matter with me that I can't be nice to his kids?"

For two days before Jason visited, I'd worry about it. His dad worked sometimes on Saturday afternoons, and he'd leave Jason with me. I looked forward to having personal time and time with my husband on my weekends off, and entertaining a ten-year-old boy wasn't high on my list. Sometimes I'd suggest that Jason could go to work with his dad. Rick felt hurt because he thought I didn't want his son around. It took us a long time to make those Saturdays work for all of us.

(JULIE, FORTY-ONE, STEPCOUPLING FOR FOUR YEARS)

Over time, you and your partner will come to agree on your job description as you're able to talk about your expectations of each other. In the interim, be patient with yourself. Ease into stepparenting by giving yourself some latitude.

Look for ways you might be trapping yourself in a role you can't handle.

The soccer games just about did me in. In the beginning, I wanted to be a good stepmother, so I went to every one. Every weekend the girls were here, we traipsed around—usually in the cold and rain—to one game after another. Chuck wanted me to go to keep him company. The girls' mom was at all the games, too, and I didn't think they needed another adult cheering.

Finally, I asked Chuck if I could please skip some games. He wasn't thrilled about it, but the first time I stayed home, it was wonderful. I took a long hot bath, then cleaned up my desk and balanced the checkbook. Those three hours made a huge difference in my weekend. I'm sure I was much more pleasant to be around.

(VALERIE, THIRTY-SIX, STEPCOUPLING FOR TWO YEARS)

Being willing to balance your individual and stepcouple needs with the requirements of being a stepparent requires a mature perspective. Learning to do so takes time.

My stepson's school conference is next week. Nobody's invited me to go; my husband, his ex, and my stepson are all going to be there. I think I deserve to go and to know what's happening at school; he spends half his time at our house, after all.

You absolutely deserve to know what's happening in your stepson's school life, and he'll be well-served by your awareness. However, whether or not you should attend his conference depends on your reason for wanting to be there and the situation.

Consider how your stepson will feel if you and his mother both attend. If the two of you have successfully attended events together in the past, he might be comfortable. If there's tension or hostility between the two of you, he'll certainly pick up on it in the small forum of a school conference. If you're committed to attending his school-related events to support him, start with a larger, less personal setting—an assembly, for instance.

Consider, too, whether your presence will detract from the purpose of the conference: to convey necessary information between parents and teacher. If you choose to show up without warning, you'll likely derail the meeting, doing an injustice to your husband, your stepson, and his teacher.

Of course you feel you deserve to attend a parent-teacher conference. If his parents have joint custody, you spend a considerable number of hours with your stepchild. If you're there when he gets home from school, you probably serve snacks and help with homework. Certainly you make invaluable contributions to your stepchild's life.

Just don't equate the importance of what you do as a stepparent with the credit you receive for it. Many stepparents feel their role goes unrecognized by the community, the school system, even their stepchild.

When Peggy married his widower father, Chad was in the fifth grade. For the next seven years, Peggy was the only mother figure in Chad's life. They don't look anything alike. He's short and stocky, she's tall and willowy. She's a brunette; he's a towhead. Yet they developed a close and trusting relationship that many mothers would envy.

When Chad went to college, Peggy missed him. Judging from his frequent phone calls, he missed her, too.

She and Chad's father flew out to visit during homecoming weekend. Chad greeted them with hugs in the lobby of his dorm, then he took them upstairs to show off his room. His half held a twin bed with a rumpled madras bedspread and a desk. A stack of textbooks and a few framed photos rested on the worn oak desktop. Peggy stepped closer for a better look.

Chad's girlfriend beamed from a wooden frame. A snapshot she'd taken of her husband during their last vacation rested next to it. The final frame held the image of Chad's biological mother, now dead for nine years.

"I was surprised and a little hurt that he didn't have a picture of me," says Peggy. "But it didn't really matter all that much. I know that he cares about me and that I gave him exactly what he needed for seven years."

Peggy knew that, had she not been in Chad's life, a different young man would have gone off to college. She also knew one of the secrets of stepparenting: cherish internal rewards.

When I met my stepdaughter, her mother indulged her with material things: clothes, CDs, whatever she asked for. That's what mother/daughter meant to them: shopping. Over time, I've talked with her and shown her some of the things about caring for people that don't have anything to do with money and things. My stepdaughter still enjoys having new things, but I also see that she can be very caring and generous with people she's fond of. That's my influence, I think.

(LINDA, THIRTY-SEVEN, STEPCOUPLING FOR EIGHT YEARS)

Some stepcouples naturally recognize and appreciate the efforts that each partner makes as a stepparent. If you'd like more appreciative comments, you may have to ask for them. Few people are practicing psychics, and asking for what you want is the best way to get it. Remember, too, that you might have to ask more than once.

Also, try focusing on what the two of you are accomplishing together.

When I feel stressed, I make it a point to start noticing what my husband does for our stepfamily. I realize how much he is doing and how hard we're both working. It's like a reality orientation for me; we're in this together.

(STEPMOM IV, TWENTY-NINE, STEPCOUPLING FOR ONE AND A HALF YEARS)

While verbal affirmation is nice, it isn't necessary for adults. As is the case with any job, knowing you've done your best is its own reward.

For many stepparents, knowing you've done your best also must be reward enough.

If my stepdaughter gets in trouble at school, they call the house. Since I work at home, I get the phone call. I always feel terrible when this happens.

Stepparents occupy a second-row seat in a child's life. They're slightly removed when there's cause for celebration. That's the bad news.

The good news? Stepparents still sit in the second row when a child screws up. The flip side of getting little credit for contributing to a child's success is bypassing blame when things go wrong.

Of course, other people may take a different view. Irate teachers, neighbors, and parents don't bother to clarify bloodlines. Over time, though, as you become clearer about your role as a stepparent, you can respond appropriately without owning the problem personally.

> *One of the very best parts about being a stepmother is having a little distance. With two kids of my own and our mutual child, it's a relief to let Lilly's mom and dad deal with the big issues in her life.*
>
> *When Lilly and her dad argue, I walk away. Why would I need to stay in the room with that kind of commotion? It works really well for me to bow out sometimes and not listen. Thank heavens it's not my problem.*
>
> (LINDA, THIRTY-SEVEN, STEPCOUPLING FOR EIGHT YEARS)

Step back from a problem and maintain support for your partner. He or she needs your encouragement and friendship. He or she may also welcome your input.

This is much easier said than done, by the way. However, compelling reasons make it worth the effort. When kids mess up, it's a rare adult who doesn't react. If both biological parents are already involved and upset, your emotional reaction fans the flames, making the situation worse for everyone.

If you're so upset that your partner must placate you, he'll have less energy to deal with his wayward child. Your strong negative reaction may make your partner focus on defending his child, preventing the real issue from being addressed. If the two of you lock horns over your stepchild's behavior, as a step-couple, you derail your ability to problem-solve.

No stepparent is like Buddha, serene in every situation. Certainly, your anger is reasonable and your hurt feelings justifiable if you're directly affected—for instance, if your person or property is intentionally damaged, your money is stolen, or you lose work time to deal with an errant child. These circumstances often represent a seriously troubled child. Take the steps needed to prevent an immediate recurrence, strongly encourage your partner to seek appropriate help for the child, and support that process as best you can. If the events take a toll on your stepcouple relationship, consider getting professional help for yourselves as well.

In order to achieve some distance from a less destructive problematic situation with your stepchild, you must hope that his or her biological parents will deal with it. If letting go is difficult for you, consider that you may need to nurture your trust in your mate's abilities as a parent. Trust is like a muscle; it strengthens with exercise.

When my stepson was in high school, his mom and I became aware that he was smoking marijuana regularly. I was very angry at my stepson and concerned for his safety.

My wife and I talked about this at length, and she said she'd take care of it. I didn't tell her how to handle it, even

though I had very strong feelings. She developed a plan,
researched it, confronted him, and got him into drug treatment.

It wasn't my job to tell her what to do with her son, but I
put a lot of energy into supporting her, listening to her, and
offering advice when she asked for it.

(STEPDAD II, FIFTY-FOUR, STEPCOUPLING
FOR FIFTEEN YEARS)

Remind yourself, too, that your stepchild's parents raised him or her before you came on the scene. You may have very strong opinions and feelings about how your stepchild should be raised, and over time you'll have the opportunity to express them. Resist the temptation to leap into the fray.

Maintain a little bit of distance and create a whole new perspective on the situation. You may find yourself taking on the role of sounding board and adviser. You can only do this if you're calm and impartial.

When my daughter and I have a hard time talking to each
other, my husband will often take me aside and point out some-
thing I hadn't thought of. He knows us both well, and he can
see things more clearly because he's not the one who's upset. It's
like having an objective parenting consultant living with me
twenty-four hours a day. I rely on his perspective.

(STEPMOM III, THIRTY-THREE, STEPCOUPLING
FOR ONE YEAR)

Before offering your perspective on a situation, be sure it's welcome. Ask your partner if he or she would like to know what you think. Honor the fact that they might not be interested in your input at the moment.

Encourage and empower your partner. Avoid blaming, lecturing, and giving unsolicited advice. Another role that you may end up including in your stepparent job description is facilitator, depending on your interest and ability.

Occasionally, Chuck and his daughter don't listen to each other very well. He'll rant and rave about something, and she'll argue with him. It's like they're having separate conversations. Once in a while I hang in there with them and make sure they're hearing each other. I'll stop them both and ask if I can say something, then rephrase what they've said and ask if I got it right. It's one way I can help my husband parent without taking sides.
(VALERIE, THIRTY-SIX, STEPCOUPLING FOR TWO YEARS)

Partners in a stepcouple can offer each other strength, encouragement, and insight during the challenging moments of parenting; this is an unheralded joy of remarriage. Working together to raise children bonds stepcouples deeply as they learn to stay calm, step back from the fray, and step up in support of one another.

When I remarried, my youngest child gained a little brother. My daughter, who's six, says she wants to be a baby again. She's sucking her thumb and talking baby talk. I'm not sure how to respond. She used to be so proud of going to kindergarten!

Combining families can mean that everyone's role changes. Single children become one of a bunch, and birth order reshuffles when stepsiblings move into a shared household.

Role displacement happens when a youngest is ousted from that position by a still younger stepsibling or an eldest becomes a middle child. Changing positions can be very difficult for children.

> When Bill and I married, my oldest son became a middle child in a family of six. Drew, my son, and Steve, Bill's son, were only a year apart and they fought constantly.
>
> One evening Bill and I went out. We returned to find that the boys had had a fistfight while we were gone. The baby-sitter was very upset.
>
> After that, though, they seemed to settle into their positions in the family. They had to fight to figure out how to be in the same household together. It was like dogs fighting to be the alpha male.
>
> After their fistfight, Steve was unkind to Drew, which was very hard on both my son and me. Over time, though, we all began to appreciate Drew's tremendous sense of humor. He put everyone in the family in stitches in a way no one else could. It was a really important job in our family, making everyone laugh, and he did it so well. Drew became more confident about himself as we all appreciated his sense of humor—even Steve.
>
> (SHARON, FIFTY-SIX, STEPCOUPLING
> FOR TWENTY-EIGHT YEARS)

Even when a child's birth order is maintained, he or she can still experience role change. Being the youngest of five children feels different from being the youngest of two. Having a little brother and a little stepsister takes some adjustment when you're used to just one small sibling in the house.

Children experience role change and displacement at the same time that they face many other stepfamily issues. Sometimes distress about displacement is more obvious, as when a child who's no longer the youngest adopts babyish behaviors.

Understanding the meaning behind your children's behavior provides clues to the most effective parenting actions.

What's a loving parent to do when a child is displaced? Your natural impulse is to protect your offspring, to fix what makes him or her unhappy. As you look for ways to do this, your spouse may suddenly seem hardhearted about your child's distress. A stepchild who's now the youngest shows signs of being intolerably immature, and the one who replaced your child as oldest strikes you as domineering and aggressive. You may lash out at your spouse or your stepchildren in anger.

Reshuffling roles is just part of creating a stepfamily. Instead of focusing on who lost what privileged position, a successful stepcouple works together to help all the children understand the process, find their unique niche in the stepfamily, and identify what they've gained, as well as what they've lost. Each partner must deal with his or her own feelings about a child's distress. If one or both partners feel angry, guilty, or resentful, they have to calm down before they can work together as a stepcouple. Adults do their emotional homework, then help children find their places.

Understanding and validating the experiences of the children in your stepfamily is a powerful first step. Your only child didn't ask for three siblings, why should she be happy to have them? How could it possibly feel right? "Of course it's hard not to be the baby anymore! Of course you don't like being younger than your new big brother; who would?"

Yet despite the obvious stress of shifting positions, each child can and must find a personal place in the stepfamily that feels comfortable. The adults in a stepcouple can ease this process by noticing when children seem unsure about how they fit in and helping them find a place. Even small acts can be symbolically huge.

We had four dining-room chairs. When all five of us sat down to eat, we'd pull in a chair from our home office. One of the older kids would sit in it.

My wife and I made a point of going out and buying two more dining room chairs. It was important to both of us that everyone have a permanent place around the table.

(STEPDAD II, FIFTY-FOUR, STEPCOUPLING
FOR FIFTEEN YEARS)

Each child also makes a unique contribution to the stepfamily, which adults acknowledge to each other, to the child, and to stepfamily members.

Gina inherited her mother's artistic abilities. She could create beautiful flower arrangements, make nametags, and set a beautiful table. She could also tell which items of clothing looked best together. We all called upon her for that. My sons thought it was really cool. She has a very good eye.

(SHARON, FIFTY-SIX, STEPCOUPLING
FOR TWENTY-EIGHT YEARS)

Despite obvious losses, there are also gains to be found. Proactive stepcouples help children gradually realize the benefits of their new positions.

Emily will tell you, if you ask her what it's like to have a little [step]sister, that she hates it. But I can see how much they enjoy playing together. Sure, they fight sometimes; what siblings don't? Over time, I think she'll say more about the fun parts.

(VALERIE, THIRTY-SIX, STEPCOUPLING FOR TWO YEARS)

Regardless of shifting birth order, all children experience role changes when they become part of a larger family unit. Fish become relatively smaller when the pond gets bigger.

Role adjustment for the children in a stepfamily takes time, just like the role adjustment for adults does. The stepcouple can ease the process by acknowledging what is, creating a shared vision of what can be, and helping all their children see the possibilities.

I was a single mother to my two daughters before I married and became a full-time parent to my husband's two children as well. I thought I could be a mother to everyone, but I'm having a hard time figuring out how to do that.

In some versions of *The Nutcracker* ballet, children tumble out from under the skirts of a larger-than-life Mother Ginger. Her relationship to them is irrelevant; she offers the same haven to all.

No stepmother believes she could be twelve feet tall, like Mother Ginger. But many believe, at least at the outset, that they can embrace all the children in their stepfamily equally.

The truth is that you have a different tie to and play a different role in the lives of each of the children in your household. You'll inevitably feel closer to and more comforting toward your own children.

I remember the first time my stepdaughter got sick. I was pretty nurturing toward my own children when they were ill; lots of sitting on the edge of the bed and brushing their hair back from their foreheads, juice and crackers and library books. I didn't know what to do with her. I wasn't comfortable mothering

*her—I'm not her mother. I'd knock on her door and ask if she
needed anything. I'd bring her what she wanted, but she never
called to me the same way my own kids did when they were
sick, so I thought maybe she just wanted to be left alone. I felt
so torn. I wanted to do more for her—and I didn't.*

*(SHARON, FIFTY-SIX, STEPCOUPLING
FOR TWENTY-EIGHT YEARS)*

Forgive yourself for feeling the way you do. Trying to force
yourself to feel differently only makes it harder. Acknowledging that you have different ties with each child in your household frees you to identify what each truly needs from you.
Maybe your stepchild doesn't need you to be a nurturer, maybe
he or she just needs someone to be there and to listen. Look
for the job that's needed instead of doing the one you think
you should.

As a stepcouple, give each other permission to have different roles in each child's life.

*After Bill and I married, one of my most important jobs was to
transport the kids. One of the ways I was able to connect with
Gina happened when I took her back and forth to the ortho-
dontist.*

*She hated having her braces tightened. It hurt. She'd be so
crabby, and I'd just listen and drive. That was one thing I knew
how to do for her: listen.*

*(SHARON, FIFTY-SIX, STEPCOUPLING
FOR TWENTY-EIGHT YEARS)*

Your role as a biological parent also changes when you
repartner and add stepchildren to your household. Now that

you're all part of a larger family, adults have less time and more needs and preferences to take into account.

> *I hated telling Beth, "You're one of five now." I felt so guilty that I didn't have the time or the energy to do the kinds of things that I used to do for her: going shopping on a moment's notice or taking her to rent a movie late at night. In our step-family, there are always two or three other people who need something, too. I just couldn't mother her the same way that I had when it was just us. She couldn't have all of me.*
>
> (JULIE, FORTY-ONE, STEPCOUPLING FOR FOUR YEARS)

Forgive yourself for these natural changes in your role as a biological parent. In essence, you took on another job when you became a stepparent. The increased demands on you reduce your flexibility with and availability to your own children.

And, remembering that it's natural to have different relationships with different children, you need to find ways to attend to your biological children's need for you. You can rub your own children's backs while they go to sleep without feeling that you have to do exactly the same for your stepchildren. You can take your own child out for a doughnut on a Saturday morning while your stepchild plays soccer.

As a stepcouple, recognize and accept the special nature of the biological parent-child tie and give each other permission to nurture it. For example, some stepfamilies have "nights out." One evening a week, parents spend a couple of hours with their biological children.

> *Tuesday night, I take one of the girls out for a hamburger. Their dad takes the other one, and Rick goes out with Jason. We're all*

back home by 8:30, and we've all had those necessary parent-child moments.

(JULIE, FORTY-ONE, STEPCOUPLING FOR FOUR YEARS)

Having different relationships with all the children in your house means you learn to dance back and forth between parent and stepparent roles. You'll stumble a few times until you get the steps down, but that's part of learning.

I feel like I have to compete with my stepdaughter to be my husband's wife. When he was single, they were very close. He took her on trips and to his business functions. Now that I'm his wife, he feels guilty about leaving her out. When he does, she's impossible to live with.

During separation, divorce, and widowhood, lonely parents may be tempted to *spousify* a child by moving them into the role of an adult companion. A girl can become a social companion for her father or an adolescent boy acts as a date for his mother. Parents turn children of the same gender into companions as well by allowing them adult privileges.

Children fall into a spousified role out of loyalty and because seeing a parent in pain profoundly distresses them. Whether they act as companion, confidant, or counselor, their role changes from that of child to caretaker.

Children who are caring for their parents aren't being properly cared for themselves. Their childlike feelings, responses, and interests become secondary to adult needs. They sacrifice a period of their childhood. And when the parent repartners, an abruptly displaced child is anxious and angry.

Here's how one teen expressed it:

My dad used to take me everywhere and show me off. Now he takes her. I've been thrown away. I don't know where I fit in his life anymore.

(RACHEL, FIFTEEN)

While it's up to the biological parent to help a displaced child rewrite his or her role, the stepcouple must model a strong and healthy adult relationship. When the child experiences the strength of a healthy stepcouple relationship over time, she can move from the position of spouse to that of a child. When both spouse roles are securely filled, a child is more free to be a child. This can be an agonizingly slow process, requiring a great deal of patience and understanding from both partners. They have to withstand the pressure of an angry child who feels displaced. A patient and calm stepparent is key to helping everyone adjust to new roles.

The challenge for the stepcouple is to move a spousified child out of that role and back into being a child by encouraging age-appropriate pursuits. The stepcouple can brainstorm suitable activities with the child. Draw on the child's suggestions: resumed hobbies, extracurricular activities, camps, renewed friendships, a part-time job. Your goal is to help your stepchild remember the age-appropriate activities he or she enjoys—and to create new ones. Help make them happen with encouragement, transportation, and money as needed.

Initially, a possessive child may find it hard to relax a vigilant stance toward a parent or let go of the special relationship they've shared. The biological parent may also find it difficult to loosen the tie. Parents often fear that their feelings toward a new partner will hurt their spousified child, so they try to stay very close with their child as they repartner. But, if they no longer focus on the child to meet emotional needs, the child regains some emotional freedom.

> *I thought I had to hold on so tight, to share everything with her. When I slowly began to let go, she seemed to thrive.*
> (STEPMOM III, THIRTY-THREE, STEPCOUPLING
> FOR ONE YEAR)

Once parent and child roles have gotten blurred, reestablishing them takes perseverance. A wise partner can gently illuminate areas of confusion, offering a valuable perspective.

The stepcouple must also deal with the feelings that come up. Regret, loss, and guilt all arise for parents who've spousified children. The biological parent must loosen or change the tie without withdrawing completely, which can be difficult. The support and understanding of a partner can help enormously.

> *Chuck was really good about helping me see that there were parts of my life my daughter didn't need to know about. And that she deserved some privacy herself.*
> (VALERIE, THIRTY-SIX, STEPCOUPLING FOR TWO YEARS)

If you're the new spouse, you'll need to address your entirely understandable anger and jealousy. Helping a previously spousified child redefine his or her role within your stepfamily takes an abundance of patience.

If your partner has a spousified child, don't take the challenge from your stepchild personally. Your partner wasn't thinking of you when he or she spousified the child. Instead, your partner felt lonely and guilty after a divorce, and he or she acted naturally. Your stepchild is less the emotional equivalent of a previous lover than a crutch that's no longer necessary.

Resist the urge to jockey for position. Competing only confirms the child's misconception that there is just one valuable role to be had in your stepfamily. Bear in mind that you're the adult, and your stepchild, no matter how mature, is still a child.

Getting your own needs met while you're dealing with this delicate situation will help. Make sure to schedule plenty of time to connect with your partner and to remember why you chose him or her. Keep the romance alive and current, reminding your spouse why he or she chose you.

A displaced child also needs an understanding friend. Stretch to nurture a friendship with the very person who challenges your position in your new family. Look for ways of connecting, instead of competing.

I had to make a friend of my stepdaughter, so we shopped. Her mother isn't into clothes or makeup or hair the way I am.

Also, I'd buy her little things: a magazine or some mascara. Just girl things that emphasized what we had in common.

(VALERIE, THIRTY-SIX, STEPCOUPLING FOR TWO YEARS)

Over time, a previously spousified child regains the luxury of being a child, leaving adult emotional responsibilities to the stepcouple.

My wife has decided that my kid is a troublemaker. She doesn't use that word, but whenever something happens and he's around, she assumes it's his fault. He's not the easiest kid in the world to raise, but I think he's pretty good.

In the beginning, stepfamilies feel complex and chaotic. People who don't know each other very well move into a single household. In an attempt to make order out of chaos, kids unconsciously find a niche, and adults validate it. Adult behavior, responses, and conversation confirm the child's position.

One child might be a troublemaker, another the good student, yet another a clown, the brat, the athlete, the responsible one, and so on. In healthy stepfamilies, children move into and out of roles as their behavior, age, or moods change. Struggling stepcouples box children into rigid roles.

Roles are assumed by and assigned to individual children based on several qualities: their personalities, talents and proclivities, gender, sibling order, needs, and physical attributes. They reflect some degree of truth. However, fixed roles and labels encourage everyone in the stepfamily to overlook, ignore, and misinterpret subtle personality traits and changing behavior.

Labels keep you from considering everything that might be going on for a particular child. They're an inaccurate mental shorthand about a complex individual, and they drive your perceptions, reactions, and behaviors toward children.

Labeling puts children into behavioral boxes. Call a child stupid or difficult or dramatic or courageous often enough, and they'll believe you. Over time, they'll persevere in the behaviors that fit "their" role.

Negative labels—troublemaker, hyperactive, obnoxious, helpless, stupid, or even ADD—obviously have negative consequences for a child's behavior and self-esteem. So do positive labels, even though they sound nicer.

After Bill and I married, three of our children went through periods of very disruptive and destructive behavior. They drove us crazy. The fourth didn't; he was our "easy" child. He was the one we could always rely on.

And he was easy. He didn't act out as a teen like the others did. He got good grades and we could always count on him to cooperate.

I think he paid a huge price for being the easy one. We praised him for being cooperative, but he didn't get as much of our attention as his sibling and stepsiblings did. In his early twenties, he went through a very hard time. He dropped out of school, did drugs—the whole nine yards.

Thinking back on it, I wish we had noticed him more and given him more of our attention. It took him longer to figure out who he is, while the kids who gave us more trouble settled down earlier in careers and families.

(SHARON, FIFTY-SIX, STEPCOUPLING

FOR TWENTY-EIGHT YEARS)

As a stepcouple, you can enrich each other's perspective on the children you live with. They're multidimensional, constantly changing, full of contradictions—and they should be.

Be alert to the language the two of you use to talk about the children in your home. Labeling can be subtle. "My child's a good student. Yours struggles." Whenever you find yourself leaping from specific observations to general descriptions about how a child *is,* be alert for the possibility of labeling and putting children in rigid roles. You're more likely to do so if you feel insecure about your stepcouple or your children, and persistent labels can signal a struggling marital relationship.

Aren't you just stating the facts?, you might ask. Yes and no. You are stating the facts—as you see them today. You can't be sure that you accurately perceive a child's experience, nor can you be sure that the facts won't change tomorrow or next year. Children's behavior and feelings can shift radically from one month to the next. As your relationship with a child endures and deepens, your own perceptions may also change.

Consider the function that labeling plays in your adult relationship and your stepfamily. It does have a function—or you wouldn't do it.

Beth's grades weren't very good for the last two years, even though I know she's quite bright and accomplished. Jason and Allison get excellent report cards. She's somehow become our stepfamily's "poor student," and all three kids know it. I think the younger kids feel more empowered around her because of it.

I don't like this dynamic; it affects our stepcouple relationship, and I don't know how to change it right now.

(JULIE, FORTY-ONE, STEPCOUPLING FOR FOUR YEARS)

The stepparent is in a unique position to help remove labels. When roles and labels are assumed and applied in *nuclear* families, they can stick longer. Biological parents share a perspective on their mutual children that can prove very difficult to shake. A stepparent, however, brings a fresh perspective to a child's characteristics and can help move a child out of a box he or she has been occupying.

Before I knew Rick, I'd thought of Allison as a real handful, obstinate and stubborn. She was a challenge, and I expected her to be difficult in most situations.

After we'd dated seriously for a few months and Rick had gotten to know a different side of Allison, he pointed out how soft she is in certain ways.

It revolutionized the way I thought about her.

(JULIE, FORTY-ONE, STEPCOUPLING FOR FOUR YEARS)

Noticing and appreciating all the dimensions of the children in your house requires effort. By doing so, though, you free them to be who they are, instead of who you *think* they are.

Both members of the stepcouple benefit from cultivating the ability to appreciate a child's many attributes. The potential for conflict over the children in a stepfamily is reduced when adults share an understanding of each child's unique and complex nature.

My stepdaughters think I'm incompetent. They tell me this in many ways. I can't change their minds, no matter what I do. I'm beginning to believe it myself!

Even the most well-intentioned and earnest stepparent can find him- or herself the object of a negative stereotype. This is a common and bewildering experience.

These labels might include stupid, incompetent, gullible, bossy, mean, selfish, unfair, fat, too old, stingy, pushover, and so on. None of them feel good, and a relatively new stepparent is bound to find them most painful.

Children label stepparents for a number of reasons. They miss their former nuclear family and displace their anger and grief at its dissolution onto a stepparent. While they may be angry at your spouse, too, they can't afford, in emotional terms, to alienate their biological parent, so you bear the brunt of their anger. This happens more often in the early stages of step-coupling.

As a stepfamily adjusts, children still have to feel negatively about a stepparent out of loyalty to their absent biological parent. Boxing a stepparent into a particular, less-than-perfect role protects this all-important blood tie.

These negative roles are hard to change. Certainly, they resist your best efforts to prove that they don't apply. You can't counter emotional logic with evidence.

So what's a stepparent—and a stepcouple—to do?

First, try very hard not to take it personally. Just because your stepchildren believe you're incompetent or stingy doesn't make it true. Remember that, even if there are elements of incompetence or tightfistedness in your personality, they don't define you as a person or a stepparent.

Not taking negative labels personally is especially challenging in the early part of your stepcouple relationship. When you're feeling insecure about your marital relationship, you're more vulnerable to believing that your stepchildren's ideas about you are true.

Second, ask for the support of your spouse without demanding that he or she change the children's behavior. If it persists and/or escalates into blatantly hostile interchanges, then the biological parent can intervene. Otherwise, what will help you the most is internal shoring-up. Ask your spouse for "deprogramming." Ask to be reminded of the specific ways you demonstrate qualities that run opposite to the negative label applied to you. Remind *yourself* about how you *are* competent, giving, kind— whatever quality your stepchildren accuse you of lacking. Remind yourself that it's your intention to be all those things.

Third, avoid putting yourself in situations where you can anticipate your stepchildren applying that negative label to you. Children, particularly pre-teens and teens, often collude with their friends, their friends' parents, teachers—anyone who lends a sympathetic ear to their view of you.

Whenever Jason's with his friends, I'm the butt of his jokes. He loves telling them how gullible I am. Even if he and I had a great time by ourselves, it's like he feels compelled to make fun of me in front of his friends. I can't tell you how this hurts.

I used to keep hoping it would be different. I'd be so surprised and so hurt every time it happened.

I finally realized that it was going to be much better for our relationship if I didn't give him the chance to make fun of me. So when his friends come over, I say hello and then I go on with whatever I'm doing. I don't avoid them, but I don't look for opportunities to hang out with them, either.

(JULIE, FORTY-ONE, STEPCOUPLING FOR FOUR YEARS)

Take heart. Over time, as your stepcouple endures and the children adjust and mature, these labels fade.

five

Blending Your
Sometimes Opposing Styles

"You say potato, I say potahto . . ." In the 1937 film classic *Shall We Dance?*, certain words took Fred Astaire and Ginger Rogers to the brink of calling the whole thing off. Songwriters George and Ira Gershwin knew something about style differences.

The parody enchants because it's absurd that any couple would break up over pronunciation. No wonder those Gershwin boys didn't write a song about different styles of communicating or spending money! The charm evaporates when the truth hurts.

Your style is your characteristic way of behaving. It's your way of moving in—and appearing to—the world around you. Imagine two people getting ready for a trip to France. One pores over guide books, studies language tapes, and plans a detailed itinerary for each day that includes a sightseeing agenda and where meals will be eaten. The other gets on the plane with a Eurailpass, a phrase book, and a vague interest in seeing a château or two.

Your style is a unique amalgamation: a bit from your family of origin, a sliver from your fifth-grade teacher, a chunk from friends and books you've read, a slice of your cultural milieu, and so forth. As you go through life, you pick up pieces that work for you and stir them into a brew that started with your basic personality style.

In short, aside from your personality and temperament, your style is learned. As a result, it's mutable. Some people, in fact, deliberately set out at one time or another to create a new way of being in the world.

> *I grew up in a blue-collar family. When I needed clothes for my first professional position, I picked them out by asking myself, "If I were a successful career woman, what would I look like? What clothes would I wear?"*
> (LINDA, THIRTY-SEVEN, STEPCOUPLING FOR EIGHT YEARS)

You may have learned how to be a spouse, a friend, a coworker, or boss in much the same way. Similarly, many young parents glean the parenting style that suits them from their past, books, and friends.

Your style must suit you. It must be compatible with your basic personality traits, such as introversion, extroversion, passivity, or assertiveness. You can also try on behaviors that aren't part of your usual mix to see how they might fit.

In fact, there are two times in life when you're apt to do this. Trying new styles is a universal phenomenon in adolescence. And after divorce, some adults go through a similar period of trying on different ways of being in the world, experiencing a greater range of behaviors than they did during their marriage. At both stages of life, this healthy experimentation is part of the process of getting to know yourself and how you fit in.

Adults who recouple while experimenting with styles may be trying to build a relationship on shifting ground. If your mate is attracted to a temporary style you're trying on, something will eventually have to give.

I met my second husband on a hike. I joined a singles group to meet people, and that was a weekend activity. I thought I might be a hiker kind of person, too. Of course, in my initial enthusiasm, I told him I loved it, but hiking didn't stick. The next spring, when he got some of his guide books out, I had to come clean and tell him that I'd rather stay home and watch a movie.

(STEPMOM I, THIRTY-SEVEN, STEPCOUPLING
FOR THREE YEARS)

Other style conflicts can arise from unresolved divorce issues. For example, when repartnering after a divorce, your natural reaction might be attraction to someone whose style is the polar opposite of your ex-spouse's. If you've had a mate who clammed up under stress, someone who gabs might be a refreshing change. Or you might choose a partner whose style is comfortingly similar to your ex's, a seeming balm to ease the hurts of divorce. If you repartner in reaction, not self-awareness, you may find that your choice grates on you later.

Even if you've worked toward resolving the issues from your divorce and spent some time getting to know yourself and refining your style, you can still anticipate some style conflicts in your stepcouple. Stepcouples hit the ground running with hot issues: communication, parenting, and finances. Each partner relies on a characteristic way of handling them.

Even when there's no obvious reason for style conflicts, they still happen:

When Bill and I met, it was instant connection for both of us. We'd been raised the same way, we liked the same things, we wanted the same things for our children. It felt like coming home; we had so much in common. We were very much in love.

It was a wonderful change from my first marriage, in which my husband and I seemed to spend all our time trying to scrape each other's rough spots away.

Still, there were—and are—things about Bill that drive me insane. Whenever one of the kids needed discipline, he made himself scarce. Don't even bother to ask him to pick up after himself. And just try to get him to carry cash instead of using a debit card. Some things about him drive me crazy.

(SHARON, FIFTY-SIX, STEPCOUPLING
FOR TWENTY-EIGHT YEARS)

There's only one way to avoid style conflicts altogether: marry yourself. Otherwise, you can count on conflicts to be one of the forces that act as a wedge between the partners in a stepcouple.

There's no right or wrong with styles. There's just what you're initially comfortable with versus what your partner is. Resolving style conflicts is easier when you keep three things in mind.

First, focus on what the two of you have in common and why you're together. Even if your styles differ radically, do you share the same goal? For instance, although you may parent differently, you both want the children who live in your home to grow into healthy, independent adults. Identifying similarities lends perspective to the landscape of differences.

Second, remember that styles are learned and can be influenced. Being married to someone who seems your total opposite can enrich your own perspective. If you're a bull in the china shop of other people's feelings, can you learn about kindness and tact from your partner? If you act like a doormat, can you learn about saying "no" and sticking to it?

Finally, learn to recognize when you're no longer dealing with a strictly stylistic issue. Style conflicts should make you annoyed or angry, not enraged. You're likely to feel surprised, but not bewildered or hurt, by stylistic differences. Here's a hypothetical style conflict in a stepcouple.

Michelle and Mark married after each had been divorced for three years. They brought two school-age children apiece to their new home. Dinnertime was chaotic, and, in an effort to impose some order, Michelle and Mark agreed on basic table manners that all the children needed to use.

Things went well until the novelty wore off. The children relapsed into eating with fingers, jumping up as soon as they were done, and talking with their mouths full. Mark dealt with this by firmly lecturing the offenders at the table; the children squirmed and fidgeted in their seats until he finished. The next night, manners didn't make it to the table, but before Mark could speak, Michelle proposed a best manners contest, with a dollar going to the winner.

After dinner, Mark and Michelle bickered about the right way to achieve the goal they wanted—through lecturing or bribery. It took a few more arguments before they agreed on a style compromise that worked for both of them. Under stress, they still slip back into their original styles.

Recognizing and exploring style differences is, over time, like riding a tandem bike. One person may prefer breakneck speed, and the other likes to pedal slowly. Tied together by chain and sprocket, you have to find a mutually agreeable rhythm to get you up the road.

When we met, we used to talk for hours. Now my husband's like a closed book when we have a problem. The more I want to talk, the less he wants to. In other ways, we get along well.

People have characteristic communication styles. Some get quiet when they're stressed; they process their thoughts and feelings internally. Others need a sympathetic ear in order to work through their emotions and responses to a stressful situation.

Different communication styles can be problematic for any couple. However, this tension is worse for a stepcouple because of the increased stress they face from stepfamily hot spots like children, ex-spouses, and money.

Pressure and anxiety can exaggerate your basic personality style. If you tend to turn inward to mull problems over, you'll withdraw more dramatically if you're stressed. Similarly, if you need to talk through your issues, anxiety will further loosen your tongue.

Remember, even when your partner's style seems utterly alien, there's no right or wrong. The key is to understand your own communication style, to accept that it's different from your partner's, and to find, together, an effective way of communicating.

Consider the following questions; ideally, do so together. Look for beliefs and behaviors you hold in common, as well as areas where you differ. Remember, first and foremost, that different does not equal wrong.

- When you're upset or trying to solve a personal problem, do you want input from others? From whom?
- Do you conceal the fact that you're upset? If so, from whom? Your spouse? Your children? Your closest friends?
- When you're stressed, what can other people do to make you feel supported and safe? What makes you feel more upset?

• When people you care about are upset, how does it
affect you? What do you do?

Understanding your style similarities and differences allows
both of you to maintain some perspective during stressful or
anxious times—when those differences are especially apparent.

*I used to clam up under stress. He wants to talk when he's
upset, and he gets more anxious when I'm quiet.*

*It's been difficult for us. The more he pushed, the more
stressed I got and the further I withdrew. The quieter I got, the
more he pushed. "Communicate with me!" he'd say. And I
didn't know how to start. It was a vicious cycle.*

*After a year or so of experimenting with ways to deal with
our differences, we learned that if he doesn't talk too much or
keep asking what I'm thinking about, it's easier for me to begin
to open up. If he stays calm and doesn't react, I can relax
enough to talk.*

*If I keep talking about mundane things to him, like what
to make for dinner or news about our friends, I move more easily into talking about what's really bothering me. I have to feel
safe talking about stuff that doesn't matter before I can bring up
the things that feel riskier to me.*

(STEPMOM II, THIRTY-FIVE, STEPCOUPLING
FOR TWO YEARS)

In a healthy stepcouple, neither partner abandons their
accustomed style on a wholesale basis. Each mate identifies one
or two behaviors that most trouble the other and agrees to
explore ways of creating gradual change. A sense of humor
really helps.

*One of the best things is if we can share a laugh about some-
thing—one of the kids or a joke. That totally derails my withdrawal. His sense of humor is such an asset in our relationship;
he can almost always make me laugh. At any rate, I don't just
clam up anymore.*

(*JULIE, FORTY-ONE, STEPCOUPLING FOR FOUR YEARS*)

If you've been withdrawn, reach out in the simplest of
ways: with a touch, eye contact, a note explaining what's going
on for you. E-mail is a wonderful invention. If you're the one
who's chattering nervously or pushing for a discussion, take
some deep breaths and back off.

Even when you're not experiencing extreme style differences, understanding your partner's—and your own—style of
communication helps you know how best to support each other.

*She just blabs whenever she has a problem that upsets her.
She'll go on and on, over and over the same stuff until she
decides what to do.*

*At first I thought she was asking me for help figuring out
what to do, so I'd make suggestions or give her advice. That
really annoyed her, because she just wanted to talk until she
decided what to do.*

*Sometimes it seems like she's repeating herself and not get-
ting anywhere. I try to be patient and listen, because it's what
works best. Eventually, she calms down.*

(*STEPDAD III, FORTY-EIGHT, STEPCOUPLING
FOR SIX YEARS*)

A successful stepcouple tolerates their differences, respect-
ing each other's less mutable basic tendencies. The tolerance
they nurture and display toward each other is just one part of

the atmosphere of inclusion and acceptance that brings rich rewards for every stepfamily member.

I can't stand it when we fight. I fought in my first marriage, and we divorced. When my wife gets angry at me, I'm afraid of what's ahead for us. I don't know how to respond.

Adults who've had a previous marriage end in divorce commonly, and mistakenly, fear that conflict leads inevitably to the end of the relationship. One of the fundamental lessons that both members of a successful stepcouple learn is that they can be in conflict, even fight, and still stay happily married. Healthy conflict in marriage is an expression of adults who feel anchored enough by their love, commitment, and connection to air their differences.

Children whose parents have divorced also need reassurance that conflict doesn't mean the end of the relationship. Especially if their biological parents fought before ending the marriage, arguments seem to signal that something's seriously wrong. In the words of a seven-year-old:

> *Now I know that it takes more than one fight to make a divorce. Divorces happen when you have many unagreements, and you're not happy together.*
>
> (HEIDI, SEVEN)

Knowing that conflict is a normal part of being in a relationship lowers the stakes in each individual argument. You become free to concentrate on the issue at hand rather than the eventual meaning of the argument for your marriage.

The best way to learn that you can be in conflict and stay married is to do it: fight, make up, and move on. The issue, then, isn't whether or not you fight. It's *how* you fight. At the end of a healthy disagreement, no hurt feelings remain, anger has been dealt with, accountability has been shared, and a stepcouple's commitment to the relationship is as strong as ever. A solution to the initial problem is sometimes, but not always, reached.

> At least my first husband and I knew how to fight. We did it all the time. We always ended up with hurt feelings, and nothing ever changed. I feel like I'm starting all over now. We have to learn how to fight with each other and stay married, because we want to.
>
> (STEPMOM IV, TWENTY-NINE, STEPCOUPLING
> FOR ONE AND A HALF YEARS)

Begin by setting ground rules. Successful stepcouples can create a mutually agreeable style of fighting.

Here are some tried-and-true techniques for keeping fights fair and as contained as possible. Consider discussing each strategy during a time when a fight isn't in the air. Include some or all in your personal conflict ground rules.

• *Express anger with respect.* No matter how furious you are, avoid name-calling and blaming. Comments like "You're so selfish," "How can you be so stupid?," or "Your child is a spoiled brat" do nothing to clarify the issue and cause wounds that are slow to heal. Inflammatory language is equally destructive; if you find certain words offensive, like profanity, agree not to use them. Avoid sarcasm and caustic digs. Exaggerated or dramatic wording doesn't help, either.

• *Stick to the issue at hand.* Agree up front on what you're arguing about and don't digress. You may be tempted to bring up past situations and events; this serves no meaningful purpose. Staying specific to the issue at hand means that you avoid general statements like "You always treat me so rudely," "You never respect my children," or "Your son completely ignores me." Statements about the issue at hand are specific: "I felt disregarded when you didn't introduce me," "I would like it if you would say hello to my kids when you come home," "I asked your son to pick up his shoes and he didn't."

• *Check your intention at the door.* Particularly in the early stages of stepcoupling, get your priorities straight. Do you want to win the argument, be right, or heal the rift between the two of you? Remember to reassure yourselves, and each other, that you're fighting in order to ultimately be close again, not to create distance and anger. Closeness after a fight can happen even if the specific issue remains unresolved.

• *All those in favor, say "I."* Talk about your own thoughts and feelings, not your partner's. "I feel left out," not "You leave me out of your life with your kids." Using personal statements helps reduce defensiveness.

• *Listen actively.* Rephrase what your partner has said to check your understanding before you respond.

> *God, how I hate having to say "I hear you saying . . ." when we're fighting. It feels so artificial, and I'd much rather just blurt out what I think, instead of what I heard him say.*
>
> *But I can't tell you the number of times it's saved our skins. In the middle of a big fight, one or the other of us remembers to use this technique. The fight deescalates, and we start listening to each other more and reacting less. It really does work.*
>
> (STEPMOM IV, TWENTY-NINE, STEPCOUPLING
> FOR ONE AND A HALF YEARS)

• *Practice selective hearing.* Listen for the point your partner is trying to make, not the words he or she is using. If needed, close your eyes—after letting your partner know why—to block negative body language. Focus on understanding your partner's point of view.

• *Watch while you fight.* Keep one eye on how well you're both sticking to the fighting style you agreed on. Watch yourself, too; notice if you're becoming too upset to play by the rules.

• *Take time outs.* Ask for a time out if one or both of you are too upset to continue, if you're straying off the topic or lapsing into hurtful language, like name-calling and blaming. Commit to having the self-control to honor a time out request from your partner. If you're still angry after a time out, go back to your corners. The purpose of a time out is to calm down, not control the outcome.

As you agree on ground rules and experience some successful arguments, fighting will lose some of its negative charge.

> *I'll never enjoy fighting. But it's better than it used to be. I never used to know, going in, how ugly it would get. Now I trust that we'll probably work something out and, no matter what, the argument will end without damage. We don't want to hurt each other. I know what kind of language to use and what I'll hear, and I know how to stop things if we're getting out of control. I trust our relationship and our process more.*
>
> *(STEPMOM IV, TWENTY-NINE, STEPCOUPLING FOR ONE AND A HALF YEARS)*

Ultimately, what successful stepcouples learn from surviving—even thriving—after fights, is that each individual is safe to express him- or herself fully. They learn that conflict, well-handled, is part of a successful long-term commitment.

My husband makes decisions without consulting me. From purchases to social plans to his kids' visitation, what I think doesn't seem to matter.

Stepcouples have valid reasons for conflict over decision-making. First, blurry lines distinguish which decisions are best made by whom. When your children share your home, do you each have a say in how much you spend on them? You and your former spouse negotiate your children's visitation schedule, but it affects everyone in your current household; whose input counts?

Also, you bring a characteristic decision-making style to your new relationship. You've been making decisions on your own for a long time. In order to understand the points of similarity and difference between your decision-making style and that of your partner, consider the following questions.

- How long have you made decisions on your own? How long have you done it jointly? Right now, are you more comfortable making decisions alone or jointly? Would you like to become more comfortable doing either?
- What kinds of decisions are you more likely to make alone? With your partner?
- How important is your spouse's input when you're trying to make a decision? Are there some decisions about which you're more likely to ask for input?

- Are there some decisions about which you'd always like your mate to ask your opinion?
- What kinds of decisions would you rather not be involved in?
- Do you make choices because they *feel* right or because you *think* they're right?
- Do you decide things impulsively or after considering all sides of a situation?

A stepcouple can be particularly troubled by decision-making differences when one partner is used to making independent choices and likes it that way, while the other is more comfortable working as a team. If this is the case, consider the reasons that underlie your style and if you're content with the ways things are. For instance, making decisions independently can simply be the way you learned to function as a child, in your first marriage, in your workplace. However, it can also be a reactive attempt to protect yourself.

My first wife made very impulsive decisions. She'd have an idea and, boom, *the next day she'd be doing it. She once bought a very expensive car on a whim.*

I felt like I was constantly just trying to keep up: financially and emotionally. After we separated, one of the first things I noticed was how good it was to have some control over my own life again.

When I remarried, I had to keep my money separate for a while. I couldn't let go.

(*STEPDAD I, FORTY-EIGHT, STEPCOUPLING FOR SIX YEARS*)

Independent decision-making can also be an attempt to avoid conflict. Rather than facing issues head on, you force your spouse to deal with the consequences of a *fait accompli*.

The opposite of a free-wheeling spouse is a partner who's afraid to make solo decisions due to low confidence or fear of making a mistake.

> *No matter what I did, my first husband had a "better" way. I'd make a decision, then he'd want to change everything.*
>
> *It took me awhile to understand that my new husband only cares about giving input on certain things—the kids, vacation agenda, bigger household projects. Everything else, whatever I decide works for him.*
>
> (STEPMOM III, THIRTY-THREE, STEPCOUPLING
> FOR ONE YEAR)

Other style differences reflect varying ways to reach a mutual goal.

> *In my first marriage, we lived pretty independent lives. I wasn't used to working as a team when Rick and I married. I wanted to work together, but I didn't know how. I literally watched how our best friends seemed to do it: what they talked about in front of us, how they decided where to go to dinner. I copied their style.*
>
> (JULIE, FORTY-ONE, STEPCOUPLING FOR FOUR YEARS)

In addition to how independently each partner makes decisions, the speed with which those choices are made differs.

> *It takes me about twenty-seven seconds to make a decision alone. But when my husband's involved, we start with a discus-*

sion about needing to make a decision. Then we decide when
we're going to sit down and talk about it.

After we finally go over all the possibilities several times, we
decide. Then, for the next few days, we revisit the decision.

(STEPMOM I, THIRTY-SEVEN, STEPCOUPLING
FOR THREE YEARS)

If you're the one who makes spur-of-the-moment decisions, consider slowing down enough to include your partner.
If you're the slowpoke, consider the possibility that not every
decision merits lengthy mulling over.

Remember, it's the process that strengthens or undermines
your stepcouple, not the outcome. Successful stepcouples find a
way to include each other in most decision-making.

**My husband is sloppy about money. He rarely balances the check-
ing account. He pays bills late. I'm itching to take the finances over
from him, but he doesn't want me to.**

When adults remarry, their styles of handling money frequently cause strife for a variety of reasons. Stepcouples often
have less to spend and a more complicated budget than first
families do; for instance, child and spousal support shrink
pocket money. Second, while first marriages tend to start out
with both partners on an even financial plane, second and sub-
sequent marriages often involve one spouse with significantly
more income, assets, obligations, or debt.

By the time you remarry, you've developed a singular financial style. Experiences from your childhood, single life as a
young adult, first marriage, divorce or death of your spouse,
and a return to single life help create your unique combination
of behaviors.

How you handle money also reflects your confidence level. If you're a woman whose divorce brought you back into the workforce after a long hiatus to raise children, you may be uncertain if you can earn a living over the long run. For that reason alone, counting pennies may be important to you. Being downsized can also teach you to be more cautious about spending.

Conversely, a high level of confidence in your earning ability may make it easier to ignore small change. You can afford an occasional overdraft charge if your income is substantial.

Consider the following questions about your financial style. Please note that this discussion can't substitute for a factual discussion about income, assets, obligations, and goals—yours and your partner's. As a stepcouple, talk about the following questions.

- Are you more comfortable with joint or separate checking accounts? Did you have joint or separate accounts in your first marriage? Did it work for you?
- Who pays what bills now? Out of what account? How well does your bill-paying system work? How fair is it?
- How do you decide what portion of the responsibility you each bear? Is the current burden of financial responsibility acceptable to both of you?
- Do you know what you each make and spend money on, other than bills?
- What do you know about the bills you each pay individually? Are you comfortable with what you know about all the financial dealings in your household?
- Do you spend money on each other's children or do you keep these costs separate? How often? Are there circumstances under which you do pay for your spouse's children? What are they?

> - How often do you review the accounts? Is this frequent enough? Too frequent?
> - Is money a problem in your relationship? How do you address the conflict?

Remember, no style is inherently wrong. Look for what you can learn and what you might be able to offer your partner. In successful stepcouples, both members can moderate their styles. Style differences can be conflicting but also complementary. Each partner can be influenced in a positive way by the other.

I put myself and my first husband through school. Being a single parent didn't feel like a financial hardship to me; I was used to counting change to take the kids to McDonald's.

When Keith and I married, he'd been in practice for fifteen years. While we both wanted the same things for our new family—good schools for the kids and a paid-off mortgage—he spent money much more freely than I did. I had to learn to let go and spend money.

On the other hand, I taught him to pay off credit cards. He'd been pretty casual about maintaining balances, and, by working together, we cut up all but two cards.

(LINDA, THIRTY-SEVEN, STEPCOUPLING
FOR EIGHT YEARS)

And from the other side of the same fence . . .

I used to spend. Nordstrom was my favorite store, and they smiled when they saw me coming. I wouldn't have been caught dead using preowned things.

Chuck, on the other hand, had always liked shopping at garage sales and secondhand stores. While I thought that was

*beneath me, I had to admit that some of the stuff he'd gotten
secondhand was pretty neat.*

*One of my purchases our first summer together was a ham-
mock for our family. It cost a whole $4. Now I go to garage
sales because I like the stuff and the bargains.*

*I also taught him that spending money on quality can be
important.*

(VALERIE, THIRTY-SIX, STEPCOUPLING FOR TWO YEARS)

Based on your discussion about financial styles, mutually
choose one area in which you disagree. Avoid selecting the
area that you clash over most often and, for now, disregard other
areas of conflict as much as you can. Your goal is to experience
the rewards of reaching a compromise and solving a relationship
issue, not to eliminate all your style differences at once. Slow
and steady progress yields lasting relationship results.

Once you've chosen an area of conflict, begin by brain-
storming a variety of ways of doing things differently. Generate
as many possibilities as you can think of, without commenting
on their merits. Consider talking to other couples about how
they handle the mechanics of finances. Then choose a solution
to try for the next few weeks or months. You may luck out and
light on the permanent solution to your style difference or you
may need to refer back to your list a time or two before ending
up with a long-term answer.

Over time, developing a mutually agreeable financial style
nurtures trust and comfort within your stepcouple relationship.
While financial style differences can bring conflict, facing them
can also eventually bring closeness and confidence.

**I want my boys to earn their spending money. My husband
hands out cash to his girls when they ask for it. We both want our**

kids to have money, but we go about giving it to them in different ways.

Children and money can be a combustible mixture in a stepfamily. No matter how together you are on other issues, when a child needs or wants money, everyone becomes aware of differences in the stepcouple. Working out a mutually acceptable compromise about how you give out money helps your stepcouple—and your children.

Differentiating financially along biological lines between children who live together keeps a stepfamily from truly melding. When Haves and Have-Nots live or spend time in the same house, tension simmers.

A spouse who hands out money because he or she has more money perpetuates the power imbalance that can occur when adults with different income and asset levels marry. A measure of power and opportunity changes hands when the dollars do.

Allowances are just one way that differing financial styles affect the children in a stepfamily. When it comes time for cars and college, the scale of conflict mushrooms. It's best by far to pinpoint and work out style differences early on.

To help you understand each other's point of view about children and money, consider using the following questions as the basis for conversation. Pick times when you're not in active conflict about the subject, and remember that your purpose is to gain perspective. You're not trying to persuade.

- How and where should children get spending money? In your stepfamily, how much do you think they should get?
- If children need money for something special, how do they get it?

- In your opinion, should your children be given most of what they need or want or should they work for it? Under what circumstances would your opinion change?
- How do you handle spending money for visiting versus residential children?
- What happens in the other household regarding money and how does it affect your style? Do the children in your home get money from grandparents and other extended family members? How does this affect your style?
- In your stepfamily, do children only get money from their biological parent or is money shared between stepparents and stepchildren?

Fairness is a worthy goal—and one that is not always possible to achieve when children move between households.

The girls' dad is very well off, and he ponies up money all the time. Beth has a closet full of clothes and she always has money at hand. Thank God Jason's not a clotheshorse. He wears the same three pairs of pants over and over—and two pairs of shoes is enough.

He's aware of the difference. It seems unfair to him, but that's the way it is.

(JULIE, FORTY-ONE, STEPCOUPLING FOR FOUR YEARS)

Even if you can't ensure equal acquisitions and opportunities because of the influence of other parents, you can take steps toward making sure that the kids in your household are treated fairly—if only in your household. If you treat the kids in your home with integrity when they're there, they can get used to standards that vary between households. If you're comfortable with the style in your home, they'll get used to it.

> *My son gets a significant allowance from his father even though he works. That's not our style. I can't control what his father gives him, and there will always be differences between our house and theirs.*
>
> (STEPMOM V, FORTY-THREE, STEPCOUPLING
> FOR ELEVEN YEARS)

Gender and age can also make a difference in the way children are treated within the same household. Explaining these reasons behind different treatment can help your stepfamily pull together.

> *Things in our house are different but fair. All the kids share kitchen duties and they have other responsibilities as well. Jason is strong enough to cut the grass, so it's part of what he has to do to earn an allowance. Allison sets the table and picks up after herself. Beth watches her sister a lot and cleans one bathroom and the basement family room.*
>
> (JULIE, FORTY-ONE, STEPCOUPLING FOR FOUR YEARS)

Pay attention, too, to how money flows between adults and children in your stepfamily. Many adults find it far easier to reach in their pocket for their own children. They may hesitate to do so for a stepchild or resent it. While these feelings are natural, successful stepcouples don't allow them to get in the way of treating all the children in the family respectfully and fairly.

Despite your best efforts, the children in your stepfamily may not agree that the situation is fair. However, your continuing focus on fairness sends a powerful message of stepfamily unity.

My husband demands that his kids do whatever he says without asking questions. I've always been more flexible with mine. We agree that we both want respectful, responsible children, but not about how to get them to be that way.

When families combine, discipline can be a major issue. Both members of a stepcouple bring parenting patterns with them. By the time adults have had children, divorced, and remarried, they're well practiced at a particular style of disciplining their children. Your discipline style encompasses all the strategies you use to try to modify your children's behavior.

Being aware of and able to express the contrasts in your parenting styles is a significant first step toward finding a way to reduce them over the long run. The following questions provide a framework for a nonconfrontational conversation about parenting. Remember, you're trying to understand each other better, not recruit a convert to your style of discipline.

- Why do children misbehave?
- When can you realistically expect your children to behave? To misbehave?
- What's your philosophy about disciplining children? Where did it come from?
- Which of the following strategies do you use most often to discipline your children? Pick your top five.

incentives	being assertive
pleading	consequences
commanding	ordering
negotiation	waiting
yielding	requesting

rewarding	punishing
bribing	resolving conflict
threatening	yelling
lecturing	relying on routines/rules
giving up	other _____
spanking	

- How well do they work for you? Are you mostly happy with the results?
- Are there tactics you'd like to use more? Which ones?
- Which would you like to use less?
- Which strategies would you never use?
- Which ones do the two of you use in common?
- Which ones don't you use in common? Where do you disagree?

Depending on your philosophy and the methods you use most often, your discipline style tends to be *autocratic, permissive,* or *authoritative.* Rather than pigeonholing your or your partner's style, reflect on what you know and how you feel about each style.

To control children, autocratic parents yell, lecture, command, order, bribe, threaten, and punish. They may also use corporal punishment. They assume the role of unquestioned boss in the family, and children may only obey and comply. Challenging parental directives is out of the question for the children of autocratic parents.

Easygoing or permissive parents offer children unlimited freedom. When the parents don't like the results, they plead, wish things were different, hope and wait for the situation to change, and eventually resign themselves to the way things are. The child follows his or her own wants and instincts. The role of an easygoing parent is to facilitate the agenda of a child who's in charge. The child makes his or her own decisions.

Authoritative parents clearly communicate their expectations and requirements to children—and use clear statements, negotiation, conflict resolution, and problem-solving skills to fine-tune them. They create incentives for desired behaviors and let children experience natural consequences. Consistent rules and routines make it easier for children in the household to do the right thing. An authoritative parent is a leader and guide, instilling responsibility and building self-esteem in children. The child's job is to think, learn, and grow.

Style conflicts can happen in stepcouples where partners share the same goals in raising children. They both want good kids, but they go about raising them in different ways.

> *Rick yells. We agree on almost everything about being parents. But he relies on yelling to get the kids—his or mine—in line. I get sharp with the kids, too, but I'm quieter.*
>
> *The yelling was one of the hardest things for my kids and me to get used to. My older daughter, in particular, had a hard time with the yelling. At first, she was afraid of him, but she learned that his bark is worse than his bite.*
>
> (JULIE, FORTY-ONE, STEPCOUPLING FOR FOUR YEARS)

Conflicting discipline styles can be alarming, especially when your children are directly affected. You may feel so anxious that the situation seems intolerable to you. Barring physical or emotional abuse of children, avoid taking dramatic steps or issuing ultimatums. As a stepcouple, focus initially on the *process* of dealing with conflicts over discipline style, rather than the outcome of eliminating them.

Discuss your differences with respect and try to avoid reacting with anger or defensiveness. Using positive communication skills, try to listen to and understand each other's points of view. Begin to turn your attention toward common ground, too. Consider which parenting strategy or strategies the two of you both use; this is the foundation of your joint parenting style. Are there other parenting tactics that you'd like to learn more about together? Read books or investigate the possibility of taking a parenting class in your community. See the reference section at the back of this book for some suggestions.

In addition to creating conflict, different discipline styles can enrich your stepfamily. Each partner can learn new ideas and behaviors from the other without abandoning the discipline style they brought to the marriage.

I've learned about listening from Julie. She listens to her girls gripe without giving in to them. She's also a great listener for Jason. I'm learning how to say less and hear more.

(RICK, FORTY-SIX, STEPCOUPLING FOR FOUR YEARS)

I learned from Rick how to expect more from my children. I was pretty lax about some of the basic responsibilities, like cleaning up after themselves and taking care of the animals. I did more than I should for them. They weren't learning to be responsible for themselves, and Rick pointed this out.

Also, I learned that children have to be taught how to behave. For instance, Jason always left a mess in the kitchen. Rick reminded me that Jason put his dishes in the dishwasher only after we asked him to start doing that. We'd never told him to clean up the crumbs and spilled juice on the counter. I just expected him to notice his mess and take care of it. His dad

taught me that Jason had to learn all the individual pieces that
go into cleaning up after himself in the kitchen.

    (*JULIE, FORTY-ONE, STEPCOUPLING FOR FOUR YEARS*)

Over time, new perceptions and discipline styles evolve.
Differences will, most likely, continue to exist. Their emotional
force, however, is tempered by the history and trust that a stepcouple lays down behind them as they travel forward through
stepfamily life.

**My children take care of their responsibilities around the house
and at school. My husband doesn't hold his kids to the same standard. Needless to say, this doesn't feel very fair to me or to my
children.**

Fairness is an issue in stepfamilies. You can count on the fact
that the children in your household are measuring their experience against everyone else's. Because stepfamilies combine
people with complex and diverse histories, children who live in
them are more likely to find evidence that things are lopsided.

Clear discrepancies in privileges and responsibilities serve
as a wedge within a stepfamily. A less-seasoned stepfamily can
break into two separate biological mini-families, based on parenting behaviors.

Frankly, my kids and I can't stand the way my husband treats
his daughters, like they're precious and fragile, like they're
princesses. Of course, they act like they can't do anything, so
they don't have to when they visit. Thank God they only come
every other weekend!

    (*STEPMOM VI, FORTY-FIVE, STEPCOUPLING*

        FOR THREE YEARS)

When markedly different expectations for children exist, a stepcouple must try to find a mutually acceptable common ground. Exactly where that ground lies matters far less than the fact that it clearly exists.

Begin by looking for a single, simple expectation that you hold in common—or one that you could consider sharing. If you're the parent who requires your children to meet responsibilities, perhaps your partner might be willing to hold his or her children accountable for the most basic one on your list: clearing their plate from the dinner table or picking up personal belongings from the family living area, for instance. You may, as you review your chore list, realize that your stepchildren are already taking care of the most basic jobs on it.

If you're the parent who treats time at home as a break from your responsibilities for your children, consider that even a single step may go a long way toward healing the rift in your stepcouple and stepfamily.

> *When my stepdaughter came to visit, her dad made her do the dishes once in a while. She hated it, felt put upon, and made her feelings very clear to all of us. But, over time, she got used to it, and acted more like she was part of the family.*
> (*VALERIE, THIRTY-SIX, STEPCOUPLING FOR TWO YEARS*)

Ideally, your common ground will be truly mutual. If one parent caves in to pressure from the other, the children will know they're being asked to make a change that their biological parent doesn't support.

> *When my dad started to nag me to clean the bathroom, I knew it wasn't his idea but my stepmom's. That really made me mad. He'd never acted that way before. I certainly didn't want to do*

what she wanted me to do. But I had no choice. I had to do it,
anyway.

(RYAN, FOURTEEN)

Children in a stepfamily know when the adults are in conflict, too. Especially in a newer and more fragile stepfamily,
they'll egg parents on, intentionally or unintentionally.

I don't do anything until my dad makes me. I see how mad my
stepmother is, but I don't care. I'm not going to do it just so
they're happy.

(RYAN, FOURTEEN)

A child's resentment of a new partner's parenting style
increases the stress on the stepcouple.

I know I'm trying to respect the good ideas that Val has about
parenting and to support her. My daughter accuses me of being
different since I remarried, though. She says I used to be nice
and now I'm not. I wish she'd just go with the program.

(CHUCK, THIRTY-NINE, STEPCOUPLING FOR TWO YEARS)

If a change in parenting style is, in fact, a mutual decision,
the biological parent must deliver that message clearly, calmly,
and consistently. Validating the change that a child experiences
is a potent first step: "Of course, things feel different. There are
changes around here." Beyond validating the changes, the biological parent in a mature stepcouple supports the decision
they reflect: "You may not like the decisions we're making, and
I understand that. But I believe in what we're doing in this
family."

Children in stepfamilies are so tuned in to fairness that even when there's an obvious reason (different ages, for instance) for different privileges, they may still see them as unfair.

Jason's fixated on the differences between what he and Beth, who's two years older, are allowed to do. No matter how much we point out that his privileges will change by the time he's seventeen, he's convinced it's because the two of them have different parents. He thinks it's grossly unfair.
(JULIE, FORTY-ONE, STEPCOUPLING FOR FOUR YEARS)

There will always be, from the children's perspective, something that seems unreasonable. Successful stepcouples work hard to correct misconceptions about unfairness, once actual injustices are addressed. The end result of this vigilance is a stepfamily that doesn't feel divided into the privileged and the underdogs.

I don't like my fifteen-year-old stepson's friends. My daughter's friends look like the good kids they are. His are creepy; I don't trust them and I don't want them in my house. My husband doesn't think it's fair to have her friends over but not his.

Adolescence can challenge stepcouples like no other developmental phase. Among other things, it's prime time for teen style variations that set your teeth on edge. Parents know the challenge of loving and supporting a child whose appearance and behavior fly in the face of everything they're comfortable with. Fortunately for biological parents, they have years of shared history with the child to draw on during these times.

Stepparents aren't so lucky. You can't connect a gothic teen with memories of the adorable toddler or eager Cub Scout

they once were. Some stepparents decide the best course of
action is to wait out the years that remain until a teen leaves
home.

> I started off thinking that I just had to endure living with her
> until she left for college. I'd get through it by ignoring the things
> I don't like and not really engaging with her.
>
> After a few months, I came to the conclusion that I wasn't
> being very fair to her or to myself. The coldness between us was
> uncomfortable. Would I want someone to just endure my child?
> No way.
> (STEPDAD I, FORTY-EIGHT, STEPCOUPLING FOR SIX YEARS)

Instead of waiting for your stepchild to grow up and move
out, you can fight the natural inclination to distance yourself.
Begin by deciding to listen.

Listening is easy to say, harder to do—to effectively listen
you have to keep your own lips sealed. Teens don't want your
opinions or reactions. They want the experience of feeling
heard while voicing their own beliefs and emotions.

> Michael was really angry for several weeks after he moved here.
> Then he settled down. Five or six months later, his mom told
> him that she'd gotten a job offer out of state and would be
> moving.
>
> He was already living here, but her move meant that he'd
> never again be in the same town where he grew up. He had old
> friends there and lots of memories.
>
> He was angry for days. I kept thinking that there might be
> something we could do to make it better. He could have his
> friends here to visit, for instance. Nothing I suggested was good
> enough, and I got very frustrated.

> *Finally, I said, "I'm sorry it's so hard for you to be here." It*
> *was like magic. His anger immediately dropped by half and*
> *slowly dissipated over the next few days. He just wanted to feel*
> *heard, I guess.*
>
> (STEPMOM II, THIRTY-FIVE, STEPCOUPLING
> FOR TWO YEARS)

So listening helps the teen in your life; what will it do for you? Most important, it allows you to gather the information you need to distinguish between a style you don't like and grounds for genuine concern. Bear in mind, though, the difference between listening and investigation.

Investigation and listening have opposite effects. Eavesdropping undermines trust; encouraging your stepteen to invite friends into your home and chatting with them in the kitchen builds it. Grilling your stepteen about sexual activity and drug use sabotages your relationship; being open to what he or she has to say about sex and drugs strengthens it. Searching a teen's bedroom without cause is a boundary violation; joining your stepteen in his or her room for a chat, movie, or video game breaks down barriers.

To reduce your temptation to investigate your stepteen's life, remember that style variations are lightyears away from truly aberrant behavior. Style variations are harmless. Harmful behaviors include alcohol/drug abuse, chronic relationship problems, anger, isolation, depression, out-of-control behavior, and school failure.

Normal adolescents experiment with styles as they try to figure out who they are and how they fit into the world. They have to try on new things, some of which are unpleasant or unattractive. Music, clothes, hair, attitude, language, behavior, friends, diet, hobbies—all are fair game for teenaged trial-and-error.

Focus on building a relationship with the very teen whose stylistic choices make you wince. Styles come and go, but the trust you build will last a lifetime.

I'm only comfortable when my home is organized, clean, and orderly. No matter what I do, I feel like our home is on the verge of being a chaotic mess. How do I cope?

Families have different styles at home. Some are loose, some more rigid, some full of humor, some dead serious. When they stepcouple, however, few adults anticipate that they're entering completely new family-style territory.

Too many players and too little regularity in stepfamilies keep them from looking, feeling, or functioning the way first families do. Children, stepchildren, joint children, spouses, ex-spouses, ex-spouses' new partners, stepsiblings, visitation, custody arrangement . . . the list of constantly changing variables goes on and on.

During my first marriage, my best friend was in the early years of a stepfamily. I'd call her and she wouldn't return my call for a couple of days or we'd try to take vacations together and she'd be weeks getting back to me because she had to check the kids' schedules and talk to their other parents.

I never understood how she could be so disorganized that a simple question like "When can you come for dinner?" took two weeks to answer.

Boy, do I get it now.

(JULIE, FORTY-ONE, STEPCOUPLING FOR FOUR YEARS)

The paradox of stepfamily life is that the rewards hide within challenges. Some stepcouples enjoy the experience of being flexible; others chafe at unpredictability.

We'll make plans for dinner on a particular day. My son James will say that he's busy, and then decide, at the last minute, to stick around. Lilly's mom will call to change her pickup time because she has to work late.

We've gotten really good at making meals that can expand and contract by one or two people because we're often not sure how many places to set until the very last minute.

(LINDA, THIRTY-SEVEN, STEPCOUPLING
FOR EIGHT YEARS)

How does the above story end? Take your pick, depending on your perspective.

Ending A: I used to have a fit if my first husband was fifteen minutes late coming home for dinner. Now I'm happy when I get a good head count. Talk about learning to be flexible!

Ending B: I get so aggravated at the last-minute changes. How can we possibly make a decent meal when everything changes all the time?

Another two-sided aspect of stepfamily life is that being inclusive can mean being chaotic.

Everybody wants to have their fingerprint, so to speak, on the house. I'm sure that's why they leave their stuff all over. Shoes, books, dishes, toys, sheet music, CDs, bikes, helmets, you name it. I never let my house look like this when I was married before.

(JULIE, FORTY-ONE, STEPCOUPLING FOR FOUR YEARS)

Again, pick your ending.

Ending A: We keep on them, but I think it's great that I've learned to relax and let things go a little more. I know that it means something to the kids when they feel some ownership throughout the house, not just in their rooms.

Ending B: I'm going to lose my mind unless these people do something to get their stuff out of my living and family room.

More versus less is one of the fundamental paradoxes of stepfamily life.

Disposable income? Free time? What are those? I vaguely remember shopping for myself and taking regular afternoon naps—that would have been in my first marriage.

My life is so much more satisfying now. I shopped to fill an emotional hole, and, while I sometimes miss a long nap, I love my work.

Things will be better when the kids are gone. I can't wait to get my house back.

Successful stepcouples frame their life together in terms of what's gained rather than what's lost through divorce and remarriage. Doing so enables them to embrace the looser style of being a family that stepcoupling brings. If your partner loses sight of the positive side of stepfamily life, gently remind him or her that the reason you're there is because you loved each other enough to risk a whole new style of being a family. There's no going back.

Regardless of the particular style of their stepfamily— adventuresome, stay-at-home, humorous, contemplative, noisy, quiet—mature stepcouples know several things to be true about life after remarriage. They've learned to be open, generous, and respectful of someone else's child. They've increased in flexibility and spontaneity. They're more tolerant, forgiving, and understanding of individual differences and shortcomings. They've learned to let go of what they can't have and to appreciate what they do have.

> *A few years ago, while I was still in my first marriage, my mother came to visit. She watched me on a stressful afternoon with my children and asked me, jokingly, to promise that I'd never have more than two. She said that seemed to be about what I could handle.*
>
> *She's too frail to visit now, but I wish she could see me flowing with three kids, two of whom are teens, a dog, a cat, and a home-based business. The contrast between what was and what is amazes me. Neither my mother nor I would ever have dreamed that I would enjoy such a messy life so much.*
>
> (JULIE, FORTY-ONE, STEPCOUPLING FOR FOUR YEARS)

I love my wife, we have a great relationship, but I hate her taste. You can't imagine what she wears and the stuff she puts in the house.

If you believe that people who fall in love should agree on all the fine points of style, invest now in human cloning research. People, even the partner you love so much, may have annoyingly different habits and preferences. They may do things in ways you'd never imagine.

> *Every time I get in the car, I have to move the seat back and turn the radio down. It's sort of irritating that he doesn't*

remember to leave the seat where he found it. But the radio? I've just about jumped out of my skin, it's so loud. He's going to be deaf before he's fifty at this rate.

My lovely wife uses toothpicks. Many times a day. And she leaves the used ones all over the house.

My husband loves red meat. I think it's disgusting. Seeing him chomping on a big, greasy burger turns my stomach.

Our first Christmas together, my husband asked, "Where's the tinsel for the tree?" I'd never even considered tinsel—it's so tacky. We must have fought for half an hour about it. By the way, we didn't use tinsel on the tree.

I like to get up early and get on with the day. He likes to sleep in whenever he can. When I want to get started on the day, it drives me insane.

He gets funny late at night. He starts getting revved up about ten, just when I'm starting to wind down.

Certain things about your partner will drive you mad. Count on it. Early in your relationship, you glossed over your partner's unappealing characteristics, overlooking, rationalizing, or minimizing them. These stylistic foibles may even be part of what initially attracted you to Mr. or Ms. Right. As time goes by, though, that endearing sense of humor turns into an inability to take anything seriously. A relaxed housekeeper looks more and more like a slob, and cleanliness morphs into an obsessive-compulsive disorder.

What matters over the long run is how you feel about and deal with the annoying aspects of your partner's style. Remarried adults have been down the road of fault-finding and resentment at least once before; they know that it can lead to a dead end. For many, experience has clarified what's important in a relationship and what isn't. Mature stepcouples accept annoying tendencies as a minor facet of a satisfying relationship.

I pick up after my husband, put his dirty clothes in the hamper and his shoes in the closet. In my first marriage, I never considered picking up after my husband. We fought about that and everything else he didn't do around the house. Now I don't mind a few clothes on the floor because the rest of our life together is so good. I know I'm not perfect, either.

He doesn't always talk to my kids exactly the way I'd like him to. Mostly, he's a terrific stepdad, and I'm very happy being married to him. I don't say anything about the little things.

I'll go to my grave before I tell my wife this, because I love her and we're staying together, but I think my first wife was a more patient parent.

These irritating habits offer you important information as well, if you pay attention to how much they bother you at any given time. They're often the first flare when trouble smolders.

I know something's wrong when the open cupboard doors start to really bug me. The problem is never really that he's leaving them open, it's something else. Maybe I haven't had enough time to myself or haven't asked for help around the house enough or he said something that hurt my feelings. When I start to resent the little things, I try to remember to stop and figure out what's really bothering me.

(MARGARET, FORTY-SIX, STEPCOUPLING
FOR EIGHT YEARS)

No relationship is a bed of roses. Or, better still, every relationship is a potential bed of roses if your skin is thick enough to tolerate an occasional thorny style difference.

six

Embracing Values: Your Own and Your Partner's

The legbone's connected to the kneebone,
the kneebone's connected to the shinbone, . . .

Think of your whole life as a human body. Your values form its skeleton. Most bone-building activity goes on in child-hood, although it continues into later years. Values, too, take shape in childhood and continue to evolve afterward. Until a bone or a value is stressed, though, you're hardly aware they exist.

Whether you're big-boned or delicate, your skeleton deter-mines your body's shape. In the same way, your individual values govern the form your life takes. Without connections, a skeleton would be a pile of bones; so, too, the relationships between your values make up a vital part of the whole structure.

What do we mean by "values"? They're whatever you feel is right and important, like love, respect, success, religion, popu-larity, integrity, hard work, generosity, traditional family values, justice, loyalty, and so on. Individuals unconsciously assign varying degrees of importance to each of these ideas and many others we haven't listed.

This process begins very early in life. Subtle and not-so-subtle messages about what mattered in your childhood home influenced your values in important ways. So did facts like your gender and sibling position and forces like your family's social class, ethnic background, and religious beliefs and practices. The larger cultural environment in which you were raised also impacted the lessons you learned at home.

Some families revere achievement, others put altruism first: Regardless of what your family of origin valued, their words and behaviors set forth a framework for life. Later, as your world expanded, you modified this value system. Experiences in school, at work, and in relationships, including your first marriage, all influence your current values.

Notice the use of the word *feel* in our definition of values. As opposed to beliefs, which reside in your brain, values live in your viscera. They're a gut-level phenomenon. Going against your values *feels* wrong, making you uneasy or anxious. Behaving in alignment with them feels right and familiar, as the following example shows.

> *Right after we got married, I had a chance to go to work in a for-profit hospital. It was an attractive opportunity with lots of income potential. We could have used the cash; we were each still paying off legal bills from our divorces. But I couldn't do it. I knew I'd be more comfortable in a nonprofit system.*
>
> (STEPDAD II, FIFTY-FOUR, STEPCOUPLING
> FOR FIFTEEN YEARS)

Your values are so fundamental to your experience that you can find it hard to put words to them. It can also be extremely hard to understand the perspective of someone with values different from yours. A person who's scrupulous about integrity wonders how a liar can look in the mirror in the morning. A person who regularly fudges the truth wonders what all the fuss is about.

Now imagine these two are married. Imagine they each have children from a previous marriage and that their children's behavior reflects their parents' differing valuations of honesty. His lie, hers don't—or vice versa. Is it any wonder that value differences seriously challenge stepcouples?

Some people think of values as an all-or-nothing phenomenon. For instance, either you value generosity or you don't. Viewing values in this way focuses on and magnifies any differences, so stepcouples would do well to find another framework for thinking about values.

Consider the notion of *value zones*. Each value zone incorporates all the experiences, beliefs, and feelings that you have about an individual concept like honesty, work, generosity, self-reliance, responsibility, propriety, and so on. An imaginary priority line exists for each value zone, and each individual feels most comfortable at a specific point along it.

The positions of two partners who feel the same about honesty might look something like this:

Honesty

_____ XX _____

Not very important   Very important

Or they might look like this:

Honesty

_____ XX _____

Not very important   Very important

Neither stepcouple is likely to experience much conflict over honesty, although the second couple may tell you your new house is lovely when they really hate it. At least they won't fight about it on the way home.

Mates who prioritize honesty differently, on the other hand, might look like this:

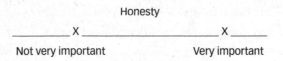

Honesty

_____ X _____ X _____

Not very important   Very important

This stepcouple is likely to have recurring arguments and silent disagreements about honesty and duplicity.

You could argue that some positions on a values line are inherently moral or right. In fact, because your own value position feels so right to you, the urge to argue on moral grounds may be irresistible. Remember, though, that your goal should be to identify the value conflict threatening your stepcouple relationship so you can reduce it or learn to live with it.

When you or your partner decides that one of you is right and one is wrong, you're drawing a line down the center of your relationship. It's a fault line in two senses. First, all the responsibility for value conflict within your relationship gets assigned to one of you. Whether voiced or silent, the message "If you saw things my way, we wouldn't have this problem" clearly identifies a partner at fault. Second, creating right and wrong sides of the tension renders your stepcouple as vulnerable to destruction as California is to the San Andreas fault.

Like styles, values can change. However, more of an investment—of energy, time, and desire—is needed to modify values than to reshape styles. Sometimes, dramatic events alter your values; when you gain a child or stepchild, for instance, you may shift to family and child-rearing some of the importance you previously attached to success. Time alters values, too, as you age or cultural values change.

> *When I was younger, I cared more about what other people thought of me and how I looked. Now I'm more concerned about how I think and feel and less with what other people think of me.*
>
> (MARGARET, FORTY-SIX, STEPCOUPLING
> FOR EIGHT YEARS)

Successful stepcouples learn that values change in the context of an ongoing relationship.

> *My husband was raised in a formal family where propriety is quite important. My background was more casual; we were more spontaneous and had fewer codes of behavior. At first, I didn't understand his and his children's strict adherence to manners at the expense of self-expression. Now, I understand and appreciate these rules for showing respect.*
>
> (SHARON, FIFTY-SIX, STEPCOUPLING
> FOR TWENTY-EIGHT YEARS)

Stepcouples face a number of value-related tasks. First, they learn to identify conflict over values. The hallmark quality of conflict over values is feeling frustrated and baffled: not understanding your partner's point of view, feeling confused, being willing to listen but not "getting it." Confusion can coexist with anger, but its presence indicates that values may be in conflict. Value conflicts recur and can become heated when issues crop up and go unaddressed for long periods of time.

Second, successful stepcouples identify the zones where their values conflict, avoiding a black-and-white view of the subject. Healthy stepcouples articulate differences and similarities; unhealthy stepcouples point blaming fingers.

Finally, when value conflicts exist, partners in a successful stepcouple try to understand each other's point of view. They also look for ways to strengthen the priorities they hold in common. Unlike styles, values are deeply held and change slowly. They're not easy to negotiate in the short run. To cope with conflict, enduring stepcouples find ways to offset tension by emphasizing *us-ness* in other areas.

Remember Mark and Michelle, the hypothetical couple from the previous chapter? Let's see what they might look like if their dinner table conflict was over values. They married after each had been divorced for three years, and both brought two school-age children into their marriage. Dinnertime was chaotic.

Mark wanted to impose order by requiring quiet table manners from all four kids. He'd been raised in a home where adults dominated the conversation during a restrained meal. Food passed from right to left, only one person spoke at a time, and children stayed at the table until excused.

Mark's proposed table manners baffled Michelle. She didn't understand why he wanted to control the children so much. Her childhood home was more relaxed. Humorous arguments often got loud as everyone tried to talk over one another. Family members filled their plates in the kitchen and hopped up to replenish them. The kids left the table when they were through eating, and the adults barely noticed.

Active mealtimes felt like home to Michelle, so she and Mark argued over what dinnertime should be like in their home. Both felt their way was best. They had the same argument repeatedly without resolving anything. She thought he'd teach the children to be uptight, boring, and rigid; he thought they'd grow into disrespectful slobs with bad manners. Only when they began to talk about what their childhood mealtimes had been like did they begin to understand why they were at such odds about family dinners.

They finally agreed that it was truly important to both of them to provide a dinner experience that everyone could enjoy and that would help their stepfamily bond together. Both realized that what they experienced as children could be improved upon. Michelle suggested that she could encourage a quieter dinnertime, and Mark agreed that if he allowed a slightly noisier experience, the children would feel more comfortable being themselves. Changing didn't feel natural to either of them, but they realized that the tension between the two of them at dinner was hard on everyone.

Some value zones trouble stepcouples more than others; these select few fill the following pages. Regardless of the specific issue at hand, stepcouples reap abundant benefits when they actively explore their value differences and strategize ways to deal with them over the long run. In this way, they reduce part of the stress on a relationship that is already complicated by nature.

I have to prod my stepkids to get them to do their schoolwork. Sometimes nothing I say makes a difference. They get Cs and Bs when they could easily get As. I'm frustrated, but my husband says they'll be fine in the long run. I don't understand how he can say that.

When your partner's viewpoint seems incomprehensible, it's likely that your values conflict. As one remarried partner says, "It's as though I'm suddenly talking to someone from another planet."

Here's the value zone priority line at issue:

School performance

_____ _____

Not very important   Very important

You can place a mark on this line to represent your own position. Use a pencil because your mark reflects your current stance, which can change. Your partner can do the same. Assume that your spouse considers his or her position as carefully as you considered yours. If you disagree with where your partner places a mark, keep your opinion to yourself. You may understand less about your partner's values than you think you do. You may also be surprised at how close to each other your marks lie.

If there's significant distance between your positions on this priority line, it will take motivation and effort to resolve. Your values and your partner's have deep roots. Set a different goal instead. Try to understand _why_ your spouse feels the way he or she does.

Values arise out of past experiences, both childhood and previous marriages, so listen for the stories behind your partner's values. Some questions follow that may help you do just that. These items explore school performance; with variations, they could apply to any value zone.

Start this conversation when you're getting along, not in the middle of a disagreement. It's hard enough to talk rationally and listen calmly to someone else's point of view when arguing. When emotions run high, the pull to refocus on the present disagreement and keep fighting can be too strong to resist. You must stick to the task at hand—focus on having a productive discussion about values.

You might hear familiar anecdotes or entirely new information. As your relationship develops, you might hear old stories in new ways. Whatever emerges as you talk, consider how it determines your partner's current position on the priority line. Cultivate curiosity about your mate's life and experiences.

Delve into your own past experiences as well. Share your experiences and how they contribute to your positions. Just as you may not understand your partner's point of view, he or she probably doesn't understand yours. You may not clearly understand your own values, either, so think of this process as a great opportunity for both of you to learn more about yourselves and each other.

- When you were a child, did you like school? Was it easy or hard?
- How important did you think school and schoolwork were?
- How important did your parents think they were?
- Did you do your schoolwork regularly? What, if anything, happened if you didn't? How did you feel about homework?
- What happened when you did a particularly good job on your schoolwork? How did you feel?
- What kind of support did you need from your parents for schoolwork? Did you get it?
- Did gender or birth order play a role in how the children in your family were treated about schoolwork?
- Did your parents graduate from high school? College? Graduate or professional school? Did you?

> • What message did you receive from your friends and
>   the larger culture about the importance of grades and
>   education? What did you learn in your first marriage?

You can't experience your spouse's perspective directly. You
can only try to understand it by listening to each other. A
single conversation is the first step toward this goal. Understanding value differences requires an open, trusting relationship, time, and the willingness to risk.

*We're yin and yang about schoolwork. I put some effort into
helping the kids in the primary grades, sitting with them while
they did spelling words. But once they hit middle school, I
stopped paying much attention.*

*Chuck makes Sarah's homework a top priority. She has to
do it as soon as she gets home from school, and he wants to see
it before she goes to bed—if he hasn't already spent time helping her. I don't understand why he's still so involved, especially
since she's almost sixteen. I think she should do it alone, and
his involvement takes time away from us.*

(VALERIE, THIRTY-SIX, STEPCOUPLING FOR TWO YEARS)

Understanding your partner's perspective is challenging—
and well worth the effort. Often, acceptance slips in on the
coattails of understanding. Respect follows, too. As your stories
emerge, you may find it easier to be sympathetic to your partner's position on the priority line.

*I hated school. I went to a parochial school because I didn't do
well in public school, and it was awful. I barely made it through
my sophomore year in college before quitting. Certainly, at six-*

teen, I never talked to my parents about homework and they never asked.

Chuck had a totally different experience. His parents were really involved in how he was doing in school, cheering him on. He won some kind of math prize in high school that they still talk about.

We feel differently about schoolwork, that's for sure. But I understand why he's so vigilant about her homework. It's a big part of what made him feel good about himself as a teenager. He wants her to have that, too, I guess.

(VALERIE, THIRTY-SIX, STEPCOUPLING FOR TWO YEARS)

When you're in the process of learning about each other's values, understanding waxes and wanes. Some days your partner's viewpoint makes perfect sense, given what you know about them. On other occasions, you may still feel like you're married to someone you don't understand at all.

Values change slowly and sometimes not at all. In value zones where the two of you are at different points on the priority line, accepting the gap between you makes it easier to live with.

In truth, acceptance sometimes proves elusive. In that case, understanding your points of view helps you better tolerate differences over the long run.

I found an exam cheat sheet my stepdaughter wrote. I mentioned the notes to my wife, who doesn't want to pursue it. I can't understand why she would just let it go.

The relationship between different value zones comes into play in stepcoupling. And some will be more important to you than others. These priorities guide your thinking and behavior, so when members of a stepcouple have different priorities, tension results.

Some value zones seem bound to conflict with others. It can be hard enough to sort out your own priorities, let alone how they jibe with someone else's. For instance, can you fully express yourself and still have harmony within your family? Does achievement require some insensitivity to the needs of others? Which is more important: integrity or achievement?

You can view conflict over value zone rankings like this:

Partner 1	Partner 2
Achievement	Integrity
Integrity	Work ethic
Work ethic	Achievement

You become conscious of the priority you assign to different values only when your ranking is a mismatch with someone else's. When one member of a stepcouple prizes integrity and the other believes that you can't play by the rules if you're going to get ahead, conflict is inevitable.

Ted has an integrity problem. He's good at sales, but he'll tell a customer one thing and then do something else. I even heard about it from someone who didn't know we were married.

I really don't like it. I know his success allows us to do many things we otherwise couldn't, but I think being someone others can count on is more important.

(MARGARET, FORTY-SIX, STEPCOUPLING
FOR EIGHT YEARS)

The process of trying to understand each other's priorities is like trying to understand how you both feel about a single value zone. It just involves more concepts. In order to have a conversation about feelings without it deteriorating into defending or attacking positions, remember to speak from your own point of view by focusing on stories from the past. While staying current in any relationship is important, your purpose now is to uncover the life story that influences values.

Be interested and curious about what your partner has to tell you. Calm your angry impulses and listen with respect. Resist the temptation to resume arguing.

If two value zones conflict, explore them individually. As you do, their relationship to each other will come into focus. This larger picture is the first step toward understanding why you feel differently. For instance, the following questions about achievement and integrity might help you gauge your partner's view of the big picture.

- How important was achievement in your childhood home?
- Did you receive any awards or recognition as a child? How did your parents respond? Were they disappointed if and when you didn't receive any when other children did?
- Would you describe your childhood family members as competitive? Did some children achieve more than others? Were they treated differently from their less successful siblings?
- As a child, were you aware of any job-related achievements or disappointments that your parents experienced? How did you learn about them? How did your parents respond?

- When and how did your parents express pride in their children? When and how did they express disappointment?
- Do you remember anyone in your family cheating? In games or sports? In school? On income taxes? In relationships? What, if anything, happened as a result?
- Did you cheat as a child? In games or sports? In school? What, if anything, happened as a result?
- Do you think your parents would have agreed with the statement that "the ends justify the means"?
- What experiences after your childhood influenced the way you feel about achievement? About integrity?

If you're willing, this conversation can increase your ability to stand in your spouse's shoes. It doesn't necessarily mean you'll eventually wear the same size, though.

My wife and I have different priorities. If she's made a commitment to do something with me, she'll put it off if something comes up at work. Whatever we were going to do has to wait until she's done with work.

I understand why she feels the way she does. Her family is full of high achievers. She wants to do well in her career and she does. I respect that.

She also hasn't been through a divorce. She doesn't understand that people are more important than work in the way I do.

I understand her priorities. That doesn't mean I like them.

(STEPDAD IV, THIRTY-ONE, STEPCOUPLING
FOR TWO YEARS)

The partners in successful stepcouples don't have radically different priorities. Nor do they always have the same top priority. Understand and learn to make allowances for what's most important to each of you.

My husband spends way too much money on his kids. He says he'd rather spend it on them while he's alive than leave it as an inheritance. But if he'd curb his spending, we could retire earlier.

Whether or not you believe that money is the root of all evil, rest assured that it *is* at the center of many stepcouple value conflicts. Money and parenting are areas of stepfamily life that involve multiple value zones. It's not surprising that many stepcouples struggle with tension about whether, when, why, and on whom to spend the financial resources that are frequently more limited in stepfamilies.

For some people, a penny saved is a penny earned. For others, spending is the reward for hard work. For some people, debt is the key to a great lifestyle; for others, it's a curse.

Thrift, gratification, generosity, gender roles, work ethic, self-reliance, responsibility . . . the list of value zones that come into play when finances are at issue seems endless. Each half of the stepcouple can disagree about every one, based on his or her experiences, beliefs, and feelings. Sound complicated? You bet it is. That's one of the reasons you will argue about it so often.

Remember, feeling baffled or confused points you to a value conflict that needs exploration. In what areas does your partner's viewpoint seem incomprehensible?

Saving money has always been a big deal to me. When I was a kid, my dad used to joke that if he needed money, he'd just *look under my mattress. When I started working, I put some-thing from every paycheck into savings. Maybe only $20, but after a few paychecks it started to add up.*

Now, Keith and I make five or six times as much money as I did when I was able to save money, and we live from pay-check to paycheck. All our kids are in private school—that's what takes our cash. We have to put anything else, from car repairs to vacations, on a credit card. We pay the cards off within a few months, but never put anything away.

He'd rather spend every dime on the kids right now than save. It's so alien to me.

(LINDA, THIRTY-SEVEN, STEPCOUPLING FOR EIGHT YEARS)

The following questions can stimulate a conversation to help you understand each other's unique perspective about money. As you get a better sense of which value zones hold the most conflict for the two of you, you can focus your conversation in that direction.

Following is a series of questions you and your partner can discuss regarding financial issues:

- As a child, were you privy to adult conversations or arguments about money? What do you remember about them?
- What were the financial stresses on your family?
- How was money spent in your childhood home? Whose needs took priority?
- Were your parents frugal or did they enjoy spending money? What did you learn from your parents about saving money? About spending it?
- How did you spend money as a child?

- Did you save money as a child? Did you do it on your own or were you required to save money by your parents? How did you feel about saving money?
- As a child, did you ever save up for an important purchase? What was that experience like for you?
- Did your parents give money to charity? If so, what kind?
- How did you receive money as a child? Through an allowance or by doing chores? Did your parents simply hand you money when you needed or wanted it?
- If you've gone to college, how was it paid for? How did you feel about that?
- Did your parents or anyone else ever bail you out of a financial mess? What did you learn from it?
- What experiences after childhood may have shaped the way you feel about money? In your previous marriage, was money an issue? Did you fight about it?
- If you were raised in a stepfamily, how was money handled? Did it feel fair to you? Do you handle money this way or differently?
- What message did you or do you receive from the larger culture about money? What do you think the larger culture endorsed when you were a child? Has it changed over time?
- What is it most important to you to spend money on? Yourself? Your home? Children? Education? Vacations? Charity? Retirement?

Understanding your points of view about a topic as tangled as money will take more than one conversation. View the first time you talk as a chance to get a glimpse of topics you might want to explore later.

As you learn more about each other's money-related value zones, you may find that previously tense topics become easier.

I used to bring up saving money with Keith. I thought we could put the kids in public school for a few years and invest the money we'd save. He never agreed, and we ended up having the same quarrel over and over. Once I put the pieces I knew about his childhood together, though, his attitude made sense.

Keith's family had a nice lifestyle, but nothing ostentatious. Then his dad left. His mom went back to work. She spent every dime she made feeding the kids and putting them through college.

That's just the way he thinks family should work. Parents make big financial sacrifices for their kids. I can respect that, and I do, but it's still important for me to put something away regularly.

He understood why it's important to me after we talked. We agreed that we'd find a way to invest $25 or $50 each month. It's much less than I think we ought to be doing, but it helps.

(LINDA, THIRTY-SEVEN, STEPCOUPLING FOR EIGHT YEARS)

Understanding why your partner's viewpoint differs from your own is just the first step toward reconciling value conflicts over the long run. However, with a complex, value-laden concept like money, a glimmer of understanding can go a long way.

Some of our differences are very painful. We just don't see eye-to-eye sometimes.

When you share the stories behind your differing value positions, you explore your differences with the goal of understanding each other's point of view. Once you've started this process, it's a good time to begin to look beyond them.

Successful stepcouples balance their differences with similarities. If value differences are one of the forces that threaten to wedge a stepcouple apart, shared values can be the glue that holds them together.

Here's how the whole process works. First, you experience the differences:

> *Bill thinks Christmas is an occasion for being hugely extravagant. He loves to be Santa Claus and make everyone's dreams come true. He loves it when our living room floor is covered with gifts.*
>
> *Christmas, to me, is about midnight Mass and a big family dinner. It's about gifts, too, and it's also a time to share what you have.*
>
> *In the beginning of our marriage, we'd have the same fight over and over. I'd say my point of view. He'd express his. Stalemate. Neither of us budged as a result of any of those fights.*
>
> (SHARON, FIFTY-SIX, STEPCOUPLING
> FOR TWENTY-EIGHT YEARS)

Then you begin to elicit the stories behind your viewpoints, using a new perspective to help you understand each other:

> *Over time we began to understand why we each feel the way we do. It makes sense that we have different points of view. His parents went all out making Christmas for their family. His mother shopped for months beforehand, and she started decorating the house right after Thanksgiving.*

My family always donated Christmas to another family who couldn't afford presents or holiday food. It meant that we had a more modest celebration, but on Christmas morning, I liked thinking about other kids unwrapping presents we'd given them. I helped pick out and wrap their gifts, so I knew what they were opening.

(SHARON, FIFTY-SIX, STEPCOUPLING FOR TWENTY-EIGHT YEARS)

Here's the next step. Take an inventory of what you both value highly. Sometimes it's closely related to the very issue you're arguing about.

Here's what finally got us out of those same old arguments about Christmas. We realized that we both wanted the experience of being generous. Bill just wanted to direct it toward our family, while I wanted to help another family. We also realized that we really shared the goal of making Christmas a family time for the kids. And we didn't want their memories of that family time to include arguments about where money was going.

I let Bill take more responsibility for shopping for our kids. I also brought home some tags from a local giving tree. Needy children make specific gift requests, and you return the tag and the gift-wrapped item. Bill also shopped for those gifts.

It wasn't overnight, but realizing how much we wanted our kids to have a great holiday experience helped us turn the corner.

(SHARON, FIFTY-SIX, STEPCOUPLING FOR TWENTY-EIGHT YEARS)

Sometimes you have to look a little further afield to find value glue.

Rick and I were raised pretty differently, so we have significant conflicts about how and where to spend money. We really only fight about them when we don't have enough to take care of our different priorities.

Even though we didn't fight about money often, it took a huge toll on our relationship when we did. We decided we didn't want our conflict to get out of hand anymore.

Now, when we feel squeezed, we remember that we've been here before. Somehow, we always manage. Calming down helps us remember what we love about being together. In addition to how much we enjoy each other's company, we love what we've done for our kids. They add to our stress at those times because they want and need things that cost money, but they also remind us of the things we do well together.

(JULIE, FORTY-ONE, STEPCOUPLING FOR FOUR YEARS)

Some stepcouples find their value glue by reflecting on what they respect and admire about each other. Other stepcouples find it in activities they both prize: hiking or biking, cooking and entertaining, renovating an old house. It matters far less what holds your stepcouple together than that something does. Once you identify your glue, emphasize it with your intention and actions.

I'm not saying it's easy to pull my attention away from what I want when I'm stressed about money. It takes every morsel of self-discipline I have. When I can do this, though, it makes all the difference in the world. We're in this together, after all.

(STEPDAD I, FORTY-EIGHT, STEPCOUPLING FOR SIX YEARS)

Love brought you together initially, and conflict is a crucial time to safeguard it. You're not likely to feel particularly loving in the middle of strife, but don't forget to behave in respectful, kind ways. Your feelings will follow the actions you take.

My twelve-year-old stepson lies. My husband doesn't discipline him; he just shrugs and says he'll outgrow it. I'm shocked that he condones lying.

Two issues may be operating when your stepchild's behavior reflects a value that conflicts with your own set of beliefs. The first is whether that behavior truly reflects a value or just a phase.

For instance, many children lie at some point. Young children experiment with escaping blame and avoiding responsibility. Some children lie because telling the truth carries too high a price. Some lie to keep up with their peers, to maintain a degree of privacy from their parents, or to get noticed. Here's another reason to consider: Your stepchild may want, consciously or not, to wedge you and your spouse apart. Any arguments about his deception could force that wedge in deeper.

One way to deal with children who lie is to acknowledge the dishonesty without raging at or shaming the child. Certainly, you need to make the child accountable by issuing appropriate consequences and to reinforce whatever truth-telling takes place. It's possible that your spouse takes this approach, viewing the devious behavior as a temporary problem.

The second issue that may be at hand has more serious consequences for a stepcouple. Sometimes your stepchildren's behavior mirrors a parental value that makes you uncomfortable. Particularly in the honeymoon phase of stepcoupling, you may more easily see values that conflict with yours in a stepchild because your love for his or her parent blinds you. If you and your spouse feel differently about truth, for instance, you're in this value zone:

Honesty

_____

Not very important   Very important

Because your own value position is so deeply held, your partner's position *feels* wrong to you. It can be very hard to remember that your partner's stance isn't wrong, it's just different. Remember, what threatens your relationship isn't your positions on the priority line; it's how you handle the gap between them. The questions that follow may help you begin to sort out the similarities and contrasts in how you each value honesty, as well as why you feel the way you do.

- As a child, when did you lie and why? How did you lie, by not telling the whole truth or fabricating falsehoods? How did you feel when you lied?
- Did you get away with lying? How did your parents respond?
- Were you ever aware that one or both of your parents were lying? To whom were they lying? Each other? Someone outside the home (a neighbor, friend, employer)? You? How often did this happen?
- Sometimes parents ask their children to lie for them. Were you ever asked to do this?
- Were there certain situations in which lying was acceptable? For instance, was it OK to lie if it meant you avoided hurting someone's feelings? Were other kinds of "little white lies" acceptable?
- What experiences after childhood have influenced your values about honesty? Was honesty an issue in your previous marriage?

> • What message did or do you receive from the larger culture about lying? Do you think it's culturally acceptable to lie?

If you have a significant value conflict, it's not the end of the world. Simply understanding your differences can relieve some of the strain on your relationship. And, over time, value differences can moderate as each spouse understands the other's story and viewpoint. Healthy partners can try on new behaviors, experience some benefit, and shift their own position.

Values change within the context of an ongoing relationship in which there is enough love and trust to risk new behaviors. The process begins with awareness that a difference exists.

When Rick started talking about my dishonesty, I had no idea what he meant. I didn't even know what honesty really was. In my first marriage, I manipulated my husband and the truth to get what I wanted. It was my version of what you did to get what you wanted in the world, and I was good at it.

It took me a long time to even become aware that there was another way of doing things, to consider that I might want to be more honest.

(JULIE, FORTY-ONE, STEPCOUPLING FOR FOUR YEARS)

The next step in the slow process of value evolution is the decision to be willing to try something different. It's important to note here that this kind of willingness comes from within; it can't be produced on request, no matter how much you wish it could.

Frankly, it had never been a huge problem until I met him. He didn't ask me to change; he only told me that he didn't feel like he could fully trust me. I knew that I trusted him to tell me the truth and how important that was to me. Maybe there was a way I could behave differently. I couldn't change—nobody can—until I was ready to and wanted to.

(JULIE, FORTY-ONE, STEPCOUPLING FOR FOUR YEARS)

Next in the process comes close observation of the other end of the priority line and trying on new behaviors. This step requires some willingness to take risks.

Then I watched Rick and other people to see how they behaved, what was truthful behavior and how it worked. I decided to try some of those behaviors: answering an uncomfortable question completely and honestly, for instance. The process wasn't natural or comfortable, but I kept with it.

(JULIE, FORTY-ONE, STEPCOUPLING FOR FOUR YEARS)

You ultimately stick with behaviors that feel right and bring good results, both in your relationship and the world.

Only then did I begin to feel the difference between telling the truth and evading it. I found that telling the truth was more peaceful than being dishonest. That niggling sense of uneasiness wasn't there, and that felt good.

Rick didn't jump up and down when I began being more truthful. The fact is, I think I had to overcome quite a bit of mistrust that he'd developed. My behavior felt massively different to me—and he sometimes registered it as just a blip on his screen. But it also paid off in other areas of my life—I became much more forthright at work, for instance.

(JULIE, FORTY-ONE, STEPCOUPLING FOR FOUR YEARS)

One or both partners can moderate their values. What determines who, if anyone, changes? Ultimately, it's a matter of openness to change and willingness to risk.

Openness and willingness exist somewhere within a successful stepcouple relationship. Healthy partners in a stepcouple recognize that moderation takes time and perseverance. It's part and parcel of developing a value framework that both can live with.

I've had my daughters half the time since their mom and I divorced two years ago. My present wife has been offered a job in another state that will double our income. If we move, I won't be able to see the girls. She really wants to pursue this job.

Conflicts over some values—for example, intimacy, parenting and money—can tear a stepcouple apart. Tom and Laurie know this.

Tom, fifty-two, divorced five years before he married Laurie, thirty-eight. He had three adolescent children; she had neither married nor had children. Laurie was an artist, and Tom's highly successful business provided financial stability and new opportunities for her.

Initially, Laurie enjoyed the perks of a higher income bracket. Tom's children lived primarily with his ex-wife, so the newlyweds were free to travel frequently on business and pleasure. They hosted dinner parties for friends and Tom's business associates and clients. Gradually, though, as the honeymoon phase of stepcoupling waned, Tom returned to the long working hours responsible for his success. Laurie returned to her studio.

She traveled with him less frequently so she could work more consistently. But she also began to experience some confusion. She didn't understand why she saw so much less of him than she had before. Nor did she understand his refusal to limit his business travels. Her discontent grew.

In response, Tom sent his wife flowers or brought home expensive gifts. Laurie felt as if his gifts and gestures were beside the point; she really wanted his physical presence. They argued more and more often, and neither understood why the other felt the way they did.

Laurie balked at entertaining, no longer willing to share her privacy and husband on the evenings he was home. Tom didn't feel he could afford to entertain clients less, so he took them to restaurants.

Tom was baffled and angry; he'd worked hard to earn a good living, he felt. His hard work was necessary to maintain their lifestyle, and he didn't understand what she was so unhappy about. Didn't he love her madly? Hadn't he given her everything he could?

Their positions became polarized, and they argued more and more frequently about his attempt to substitute money and gifts for time. By the time they sought counseling, Laurie resented what she called Tom's "misplaced priorities." She felt he expected her to wait around until he had time for their relationship. He couldn't understand her lack of support for his business. During counseling, they explored the origins of their conflicting values.

Tom grew up in an upwardly mobile family. His father started the business that Tom now ran, and the whole family enjoyed the trimmings of its rapid success. As his income grew, Tom's dad frequently brought home gifts to compensate for the amount of time he spent establishing the business. Everyone at home loved watching Tom's dad walk in the house with an armful of packages.

Laurie's family, on the other hand, had been contentedly middle class. Both her parents taught high school, and they shared a common interest in gardening, spending weekends together planting, pruning, and weeding.

Ultimately, Tom and Laurie didn't reconcile their different values. Neither had much interest in modifying their own point of view for the benefit of their commitment to each other. They divorced. Tom and Laurie lacked the crucial elements that can save a stepcouple facing a significant value conflict: a shared value and a willingness to change.

When a stepcouple takes an inventory of their individual values and goals and finds little or no overlap between their personal lists, they must create a shared value. More numerous and/or stronger wedges pushing you apart mean that you have to create powerful stepcouple glue.

Occasionally, our differences seem intolerable. One thing keeps us together at that point. We thought really long and hard about whether we were ready to pledge our lives to each other before deciding to get married. Putting it that way sounds corny, but we'd both been divorced, so we thought about getting married long and hard.

Keeping promises isn't always easy or even comfortable. For instance, raising our kids is far from fun sometimes. Especially as they get older and more challenging, I'm not sure I'm made of the right stuff to be a parent or a stepparent. I yearn sometimes to walk away from my obligations.

But I can't. Nor can we walk away from the promise we made when we got married, much as I want to sometimes.

It wouldn't feel right. Sometimes staying feels awful, too, but it's honorable, at least. We don't think that you can break a

*promise because keeping it is too hard. It doesn't happen much,
but occasionally we rely on that belief to keep us together.*
(STEPMOM III, THIRTY-THREE, STEPCOUPLING
FOR ONE YEAR)

A stepcouple with a strong shared value of staying together
can handle other value conflicts more easily. If you decide your
top priority is to keep your relationship intact, you can find
long-term solutions to tension over values. You may decide to
accept and live with the conflicts. Exploring your partner's
value stance for behaviors and beliefs that you can adopt over
time becomes a real possibility when you know you're in your
stepcouple for the duration.

Significant value conflict seriously challenges a stepcouple.
However, willingness opens the way to enduring success.

**My wife has joint custody of my stepson, who goes back and forth
between our house and his father's every two weeks. His father
and his new wife are very religious. I have nothing against God,
but they go overboard. I'm worried about what they're doing
to him.**

Value differences between two households, when a child
goes back and forth, perplex many parents and stepparents.
While you can work to understand your mate's value viewpoint, it's unlikely that you'll have—or want—the same
opportunity with the other parent in your stepchild's life.

What's a stepcouple to do? First, don't panic. Rome wasn't
built in a day, nor are a child's values. Barring any genuinely
physically or emotionally harmful behaviors, you need only to
balance your stepchild's experience and provide another point

of view. It's critical that your stepchild understand that, while you aren't comfortable with his or her parent's values, you aren't condemning them.

This takes restraint.

Sarah's mom thinks religion is a crutch for people who are too weak to face life on their own. She doesn't mince words with her about how ridiculous it is that we're church people.

I want to fight right back. I'm really mad that she's prejudicing Sarah against our values. How can she possibly go into Bible group with an open mind? But we don't say anything like that. We just say that we understand how her mom feels, and that's not the way we feel. That's not at all what I'd like to say, but that's what I say.

(CHUCK, THIRTY-NINE, STEPCOUPLING FOR TWO YEARS)

Another challenge facing a stepcouple whose child brings home conflicting values from the other household is to separate, as much as possible, value differences from other divorce-related conflict. Keep your eye on the right target. If your partner and his or her ex-spouse are also at odds over custody or support, don't lump all your stepchild's parent's negative qualities under the banner "Bad Parent." As a stepparent, the most valuable contribution you can make to your stepchild's long-term emotional health is to give him or her permission to love and honor both parents.

If you're the one experiencing value differences with your ex-spouse, continue to work on any lingering divorce issues: separating emotionally, letting go, and achieving autonomy. Displacing resentment, hurt, or rage from your divorce onto value conflicts is like pouring gasoline onto a small fire.

Nobody said this would be an easy thing to do.

After we divorced, Mike got more and more involved with humanitarian causes. The summer before our oldest child graduated from high school, he took him on vacation—to a mission in Africa. He wanted our son to understand how most of the world lives.

I thought he was insane. There was armed conflict in the area, and he wanted to take our son there. What appeal could that kind of a trip possibly have for a teen?

Mike's blind to how his zeal affects others. When we were married, he could never see that I might want something different from him. He just assumes that his being involved with a "good cause" justifies everything. That's why I left him.

Did I share my feelings with our son? No.

(STEPMOM *VII,* FIFTY-THREE, STEPCOUPLING
FOR EIGHTEEN YEARS)

If you make it clear that you think the values in the "other" house are wrong, you put the child in the position of being pulled between two points of view. Remember that when conflict escalates, children lose the most. Children can't choose one parental viewpoint over another without sacrificing part of themselves. They pay a high price when you place your value position in direct opposition to the one in the other household.

But that doesn't mean you have to roll over and play dead. Confirm the experiences your child or stepchild has in the other household without labeling them or the other adult's behavior as negative. Then, without pontificating, demonstrate the values you'd prefer in your household.

Sarah won't take a turn saying grace at the dinner table. And she kind of cringes when we use some of the vocabulary from church. Her dad used to encourage her to say grace. That only made it worse. Now we just carry on, including her where she'll let us.

Her dad really hopes that Sarah will develop a personal faith. Maybe she will, maybe she won't. All she can handle right now is seeing how some people incorporate religion into their lives, so that's what we provide.

(VALERIE, THIRTY-SIX, STEPCOUPLING FOR TWO YEARS)

When children are confronted with differing values, it expands their perspective on life. Some would argue that it even enables them to make positive value choices of their own later on.

The values your children and stepchildren eventually live by develop over time. Even when children are exposed to a consistent value framework, they often stray from it, at least during adolescence. Your tolerance plants seeds that take years to mature, and your restraint waters them.

I'm so torn between the two most important people in my life: my child and my new husband. It seems like I can't attend to either relationship without sacrificing some part of the other. What do I do to keep from going crazy?

Feeling torn is a universal experience, particularly in the beginning years of stepcoupling. The internal value conflict that you're experiencing can be painful.

You learned earlier that you rank values in terms of their priority. This process, carried out unconsciously, is the foundation for your decision-making. Feelings of being torn between parenting and partnering reflect two values jostling for top position.

Making the process as conscious as you can helps. Look first at why you feel pulled in both directions. You'll be better able to make choices that you can live with after doing so.

Consider the experiences, feelings, and beliefs that contribute to the importance you place on child-rearing and coupling. What's your position on the priority lines below?

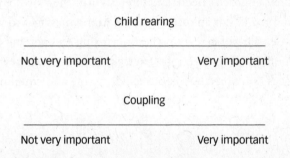

Child rearing

Not very important   Very important

Coupling

Not very important   Very important

Many people find that their value stance about child-rearing and coupling is a function of personal history and cultural environment. Your childhood experiences partially determine your position.

- How important was child-rearing to your parents?
- Were they active parents or did they get involved only when they had to?
- How did they value their relationship relative to their parenting responsibilities? Did they travel or go out as a couple frequently? Rarely? Were they more available to each other or to the children?
- What do you remember hearing about parenting and being in an adult love relationship from your parents?
- What experiences after childhood influenced the relative importance you place on coupling and child-rearing?

> Was one more important than the other in your first
> marriage?

The culture around you also influences the value you place
on your parenting activities. Particularly for women, the drive to
value their children's needs and interests over their own is cultur-
ally reinforced. Our culture also sends strong messages to women
about the value of caregiving and nurturing feelings and behaviors. The following questions can help you sort out the cultural
influences on your values about child-rearing and coupling.

> • As a child, did you know any childless adults? Were
>   they single? What were their lives like? Did you
>   know any mothers who had significant interests or
>   activities apart from child-rearing? Did you know
>   any fathers who were primary caregivers to their
>   children?
> • If your parents both worked, who stayed home with
>   you if you were ill? How was it decided?
> • When you were a child, who did you admire as a par-
>   ent? Was there a couple you admired?
> • When you were a child, what did you fantasize about
>   being an adult? Did you imagine your primary role as
>   a parent or a partner or both?

When you stepcouple, the sudden, unexpected conflict
between parenting and partnering is uniquely stressful. One
reason is that your new mate doesn't place as high a priority on
your children's needs as you do. This is a normal and natural
part of stepparenting.

When I remarried, I expected my husband to feel about my children the way their father does. I was taken aback that he seemed a little impatient when I focused on them. But it makes perfect sense, actually. They're not his kids.

(STEPMOM IV, TWENTY-NINE, STEPCOUPLING FOR ONE
AND A HALF YEARS)

When you stepcouple, there's no grace period. Coming together means that you *all* come together: adults, kids, pets, mortgages, ex-spouses—the whole cast and crew. There's no period of partnering without children to defuse or adjust to the value conflict you face. If you both have joint physical custody and the same visitation schedule, you may have regular weekends alone; otherwise, your value conflict goes unrelieved.

You experience values on a gut level. Acting in alignment with your values *feels* right. Acting out of alignment with them feels wrong. When you're torn between two values, acting in alignment with either doesn't feel right. Attending to your new relationship feels like shortchanging your child, and paying attention to your child feels like your love life is getting the short end of the stick.

I remember it so vividly. Nothing I did felt right. I'd go out with Rick and then think about how I should be home with the girls. I'd spend time with the girls, knowing that I was sacrificing some quiet time with him. There was no place that felt just right for a long time.

(JULIE, FORTY-ONE, STEPCOUPLING FOR FOUR YEARS)

When you can't depend on your gut to guide you, engage your brain. You deserve to and can have both of the things you value. To do so, you'll have to get clear about what's most important to you about each.

Clarify your parenting values. What about being a parent is non-negotiable for you? Is it sitting down for dinner with your children every night? Wiping away tears and putting on bandages? Disciplining your children? Listening to teenaged sorrows? Singing lullabies or reading stories?

Conversely, are there some things you're doing that have lost value for you? Checking homework or doing laundry for children who are ready to be more independent? Cooking comfort food? Pushing a reluctant child through one more soccer season?

As you take this opportunity to refine what being a parent includes for you, you may find that you can create more room for your adult relationship. You may not, but at least you'll know that you're focusing on what's truly important to you as a parent.

Quantify your intimacy and sexual needs and know what meets them. Talk to others who've been down this path and find out how they resolved the conflict between parenting and partnering.

The parenting versus coupling conflict didn't appear in the fairy-tale stories of *happily ever after* that you grew up with. You may not ever be able to completely resolve it. However, being more aware of your internal tension between coupling and child-rearing helps you reduce it.

I don't like the word *step*. Stepfamily, stepparent, stepchild—I don't use any of these.

Some people think "step" is the problem, that it infers a relationship one step removed from the real thing.

Stepfamilies differ from nuclear families in numerous significant ways, and stepcouples face very different challenges than do two childless people when they marry. No word in any language used anywhere on the planet can erase those differences.

Many people rank "family" high on their list of values. Here's an important question to consider if you're uncomfortable using "step" to describe yours. Does your life fit what you feel "family" means? These questions can help you explore this value zone.

> • What went on in your childhood home that meant "family" to you? Who was present? What activities were you engaged in?
> • As a child, were you in a stepfamily or did you know anyone in a stepfamily? What did you learn about stepfamilies?
> • Did your parents know anyone who was in a stepfamily? What did you learn about stepfamilies from your parents?
> • What experiences after childhood helped shape your values about families and stepfamilies?
> • Were you part of a stepcouple before this marriage? What was that experience like for you?

As you become aware of what "family" means to you, you can consciously emphasize those aspects of your current situation. There may also be some inconsistencies between your stepfamily experience and your family values, although healthy stepcouples find far more agreement than disagreement between their values and their lives.

One or both adults in a stepcouple may find themselves in a constellation that runs counter to their own values about family. They may resist embracing the "stepness" of their family

with the use of the prefix *step*. They may feel nostalgic about
their nuclear family experiences and wish their stepfamily
could feel more like one.

Other adults are more personally comfortable with the
nature of a stepfamily and embrace it wholeheartedly. They
still may find themselves challenged talking about it.

> *We don't have a problem using "step" with each other. We even*
> *talk about our "stepdog."*
>
> *Recently, we ran into an acquaintance of mine at the mall.*
> *When I introduced Jason, "stepson" stuck in my throat. It felt*
> *so awkward. I'm sure I even blushed.*
>
> *In the car, I asked him how he'd like me to introduce him to*
> *people. Stepson. I asked his dad how he thought I should intro-*
> *duce Jason. Stepson.*
>
> *Clearly, I was the only one with the problem. I realized,*
> *too, that I referred to him only by name with some people, not*
> *using "stepson" the same way I'd use "son" conversationally.*
>
> (JULIE, FORTY-ONE, STEPCOUPLING FOR FOUR YEARS)

During the 1990s, stepfamilies came out of the closet, so to
speak, crossing the cultural barrier from private life into main-
stream books and movies. Even so, living in one doesn't necessarily mean that you feel it measures up to the societal standard
for "family." Discomfort with "step" can also reflect a conflict
between your values about family and those of the culture
around you.

> *When I'm talking to somebody who's in one, I have no prob-*
> *lem talking "step" talk. When the other person is single or part*
> *of a nuclear family, though, I have the hardest time using*

"step." For me, my life is fine. It's everybody else that I'm apparently worried about.

(STEPMOM I, THIRTY-SEVEN, STEPCOUPLING
FOR THREE YEARS)

There is no right or wrong vocabulary for talking about stepfamilies. Just be aware that if you don't like the word, you may be experiencing some internal or external value conflict about your life in a stepcouple.

My wife and I love each other very much, but we have different values on a number of subjects: work, money, even parenting. We've agreed to disagree for now, but I'm wondering how this might affect our kids.

Values form early in life and are reinforced over time, so how you handle value conflicts within your stepcouple impacts the children in your household. Partners who've learned why they disagree by exploring and understanding each other's life stories are less tense and, therefore, in the best position to minimize the tension their children and stepchildren experience.

Most children observe astutely. Even if they can't articulate them well, the children in your stepfamily know about your differences. They pick up cues from you and your mate about whether these differences are disturbing or of little consequence.

For children in a stepfamily, discomfort comes not from value differences between adults but from how they handle those differences. And how you handle your differences teaches your children volumes about empathy, tolerance, and acceptance.

Put bluntly, be aware that your children are in value school. You're the teachers. Your children learn from everything you say and do—whether or not you want them to. They not only learn about how to handle value differences, they learn about the values that each adult's behavior mirrors.

> *Early in our relationship, I was pretty uncomfortable about what my daughter might learn from me. We weren't married yet; we hadn't even talked about it at that point. And while I knew there were important differences between having sex outside of marriage at forty-three and at sixteen, I was doing something I didn't want her to do.*
>
> *I knew that if our relationship was going to last, being together less would make it harder but not impossible. I knew that, if this relationship didn't last, I'd regret not doing what was right by my daughter.*
>
> *It was a hard year. I could get away in the evenings, but I only spent a few nights at his house—when she was away for the weekend. If he came here, he slept in the guest room. She never saw us get into or out of the same bed.*
>
> *Before we decided to get married, there were times when I was sure we'd break up. I was so glad I'd insisted on doing things the way we did.*
>
> (STEPMOM VI, FORTY-FIVE, STEPCOUPLING
> FOR THREE YEARS)

If you hid premarital sex, it was because you knew your children and stepchildren were learning from your behavior. They haven't stopped.

> *In the beginning, we fought openly about money. I cringe to think of the arguments the kids heard. I didn't even try to hide my contempt for what I thought was his screwed-up value system. It took us a while to understand our different backgrounds*

about money and to come to peace with them. My oldest daughter is stubborn and inflexible about money. I can't say that what she overheard caused this, but it didn't help.

(STEPMOM V, FORTY-THREE, STEPCOUPLING
FOR ELEVEN YEARS)

Acknowledge that value differences exist between you when they come up. Your children and stepchildren already ...ow how you disagree. Confirming their perceptions teaches them to trust their experience: "We feel differently about money, but we're working on it and we love each other."

Try to separate your value differences from any other conflicts you might be experiencing. Easy to say, not so easy to do.

We learned to keep our arguments focused on the issue at hand. It's a natural temptation to bring up other irritating things, but that makes a big mess. If either one of us brings up something unrelated, we say we'll deal with that topic at another time. Keeping clear about what we're arguing about makes it easier to resolve.

(STEPMOM V, FORTY-THREE, STEPCOUPLING
FOR ELEVEN YEARS)

Keeping your disagreement to the issue at hand helps you acknowledge your differences without pointing blaming fingers. If the two of you haven't assigned right or wrong to your positions, you'll have no reason to communicate that to the children in your stepfamily. Saying "We disagree" conveys a different message than "I disagree with your stepmother."

Ultimately, you're teaching your children and stepchildren that mature adults have different values and tolerate them. Not only does that give them a model for adult behavior, it also helps them learn to expect that their own eventual value choices will be tolerated.

Successful stepcouples put up with or accept the differences among the members of their stepfamily. They know that one of the many blessings that stepfamilies can provide to children is a broader and more inclusive view of life.

seven

Empowering Everyone—The Key to Stepcoupling Success

Generators make power. A hydroelectric plant transforms water power into electricity, a nuclear reactor splits atoms and creates energy, a portable generator converts fossil fuel into more useful voltage. Generators also consume power; efficient ones run on less energy and make more available down the line.

Your stepcouple is a generator, too, creating and consuming energy. "Energy," in this context, means emotional power like attention, affection, caring, support, patience, love, and flexibility. These reserves allow you to nurture people you care about and cope with stress.

Healthy stepcouples produce far more power than they use, making energy available to a system that includes children, extended family, jobs, ex-spouses, household tasks, pets, friendships. All these facets of life require varying amounts of your stepcouple energy.

One of your power-related tasks is to make sure your stepcouple energy is reasonably distributed across the whole system. You create and consume a relatively fixed amount of power, so any increased demands draw energy away from some other part of the system. When a child is ill, for instance, you divert energy from something else to provide care. For a few days or weeks, you can cope. If the imbalance persists much longer than that, the whole system is stressed. It's a stepfamily energy brownout.

The whole system is also stressed when a stepcouple struggles. They consume so much of the available power that little remains for anyone or anything else. Again, over the short term, your stepfamily can cope. However, when a stepcouple regularly devours energy, the whole system suffers. Often, children's needs are sacrificed to the power demands of the stepcouple.

What makes a stepcouple drain energy over a long period of time? Certainly, serious injury or illness, job loss, or other catastrophes require sustained energy. However, in the absence of any obvious external reason, people who have high emotional energy needs are usually wrestling with unresolved emotional issues.

We all have unresolved emotional issues; they're part and parcel of the human experience. However, some unfinished emotional business creates such a deep hole in people that it drains energy from everyone else in the family.

The energy-draining, emotional issues can be related to present events; for example, children in stepfamilies commonly wrestle with anger, hurt, and loss they can't express. Adults can also have unresolved emotional business over present issues; silent anger or cold withdrawal indicate conflict that has yet to be addressed. However, adults wrestle far more deeply with hurt and loss left over from the past and previous relationships. These energy drains can threaten the stepcouple's and stepfamily's stability.

There are many sources of past pain. Emotional or physical abuse, neglect or abandonment, betrayal, illness and death of a parent or other loved one can all cause wounds that endure for years, affecting emotional responses and relationships. Some pain persists because it's simply too enormous to forget; for example, losing a parent as a child or living with an alcoholic parent has a lifelong impact.

Pain that drains stepcouple energy can originate in more mundane events, too. It lingers because you were unable to cope with the original experience.

One of my most hurtful memories happened in the blink of an eye, when I was six. I ran home to my mother for comfort because some older kids had been viciously teasing me. I was terrified, and I desperately needed to be near her and feel safe. She just told me to calm down and went back to whatever she'd been doing.

I was devastated. I felt so alone. I remember that I went into my closet, shut the door, and laid down on the floor. The light was off, and I felt dead. It was an improvement over the hurt.

(STEPMOM III, THIRTY-THREE, STEPCOUPLING

FOR ONE YEAR)

You may vividly recall the painful experiences or bury these memories so deeply that you're not aware they exist. Then some circumstance triggers the memories. Something subconsciously reminds you of the original trauma; without being aware that you're doing so, you respond as though you're still having the original experience.

When I'm hurting, I find someplace to be alone. The more I hurt, the farther away I want to get from everyone. I realize I've spent the last twenty-seven years not needing anyone.

(STEPMOM III, THIRTY-THREE, STEPCOUPLING

FOR ONE YEAR)

When a present event triggers a response greater than or different from what it deserves, unfinished emotional business is often at work. Feeling sad when happiness makes more sense, for instance, means you're responding to something other than the present circumstances. Highly emotional reactions are often the smoking gun of unresolved issues. Rage, for instance, is a dead giveaway.

> *Even while I'm pushing everyone away and isolating myself, I'm livid with my husband for not knowing what I need and coming to my rescue. It's crazy—I desperately want him to comfort me, but I never let him get close enough to make me feel better. He doesn't know what to do.*
>
> (STEPMOM III, THIRTY-THREE, STEPCOUPLING
> FOR ONE YEAR)

As a rule, remarried adults wrestle more with unfinished emotional business than do adults marrying for the first time. Unresolved issues arise from past relationships. When you marry for the second time, you tote along the issues you had on your first trip down the aisle, as well as any that have arisen since. Until you address it, unfinished business adds to your emotional baggage.

Successful stepcouples recognize the impact the past can have on the present. Four strengths, which are discussed below, enable stepcouples to resolve outstanding issues and balance power within their stepfamily energy system.

Identifying Unresolved Issues

First, successful stepcouples can tell when they're dealing with an unresolved emotional issue. Unfinished business causes highly reactive tension: raging, weeping, storming around, defensiveness, icy withdrawal. Intense, out-of-proportion emotions flare quickly. A primitive urge to fight or flee is a telltale sign.

Conflict involving unfinished emotional business repeats and becomes a theme of your stepcouple relationship. It's also highly personal. You feel so threatened by the looming pain that you instinctively attack your partner for causing it. The message "How could you do this to me?" underlies unfinished business.

Knowing Who Has to Resolve the Issue

Second, successful stepcouples learn that the responsibility for resolving an outstanding emotional issue belongs primarily to the partner who's experiencing it. Unfinished emotional business is rooted in the individual's history and plays out in the stepcouple. Healthy stepcouples have also learned that both partners bring unfinished emotional business to the relationship.

Having a Strong Enough Relationship to Withstand the Issue

Next, enduring stepcouples also rely on their solid bond to provide the foundation from which painful issues can be explored. They develop strategies for putting out the flames so that insight and healing can replace reaction. In short, they handle the heat without letting it melt the connection between them.

Being Open to Change

Finally, willingness to change and to be open and risk exploring painful territory are hallmark characteristics of successful stepcouples. Both partners may share these learned qualities from the beginning or one might lead the way, demonstrating the growth and peace that ultimately result. However, the above traits are always present in a healthy stepcouple.

Michelle and Mark, the hypothetical stepcouple from the last two chapters, showed us what style and value conflicts might look like around the stepfamily dinner table. Here's how the story would play out if their unfinished emotional business prevailed.

After having been divorced for three years, Mark and Michelle's new stepfamily included four school-aged children. They agreed that a family dinnertime was important despite everyone's full schedule.

Mark, however, insisted on a quiet dinnertime. He liked to talk about the intricacies of his workday, recounting conversations he'd had with clients or reciting account details. He expected everyone at the table to give him their full attention.

The children weren't allowed to talk while he was speaking. If they did, he occasionally got angry enough to bang his fist on the table, rattling the tableware. When Michelle mentioned that she thought his responses were inappropriate, he blew up at her, accusing her of not supporting him.

Michelle hoped her husband's behavior would change over time; she loved him dearly and enjoyed their relationship in many other ways. In the meantime, however, she coached her own children about how to avoid making their stepfather angry.

Mark's impatience continued to be a problem. In fact, it took less and less to set him off. One evening, he shouted at Michelle's younger daughter at the table.

His wife put her foot down. She suggested that, for a while, the two of them could eat dinner after the children had finished. She reminded Mark how much she loved him and that she supported him, even though she couldn't condone the way he was treating her children.

Mark and Michelle started eating after the children went to bed; he began to relax during their uninterrupted conversations. One night, they began to talk about family dinners in their childhood homes. Mark disclosed stories of how he and his brothers had eaten dinner in total silence while his father talked.

A few evenings later, Mark mentioned that he'd recalled a nearly forgotten event from his childhood. One evening, as a small boy, he spilled his milk. His father exploded with rage, unleashing a torrent of verbal abuse at Mark for his carelessness and sending him away from the table. In fact, Mark remembered, his father had become enraged often, unpredictably, and with little provocation.

Over time, Mark talked more about how frightening his father had been. Michelle listened patiently. Mark realized that he'd been imitating behaviors he hated in his own father. He also realized that he scared their children. The family started eating together again, and, while he still preferred to use that time for talking about work, Mark better tolerated other topics, as well as interruptions from the children.

Mark's willingness to explore his own emotional territory and Michelle's willingness to tolerate this process and support it by listening indicate their fundamental strength as a stepcouple. The result was that Mark no longer needed such rigid control over everyone's behavior. More of the energy at the dinner table could go to other stepfamily members. Power was redistributed in a more balanced way.

Unresolved emotional issues must be addressed. Unfinished business—and the power imbalances it creates—is the most divisive force threatening a stepcouple. Put another way, the painful past drains power from a stepcouple, endangering their future together.

My second husband is selfish and inconsiderate. I guess I have bad luck finding good men. I don't want to put my children through another divorce, but I really can't tolerate him much longer.

If you lived on a desert island, you'd never experience your emotional issues. Unfinished business comes up in relationships with other people. Coupling and parenting place more emotional demands on you than any other relationships. They also offer you the greatest opportunities for personal growth.

If relationships are a school for personal growth, you earn a Ph.D. in a successful stepcouple. More people and stresses demand increased flexibility, generosity, and maturity, all of which stem from self-awareness.

A crucial part of developing self-awareness is exploring and understanding the energy-consuming parts of your past that you carry with you. Everyone has unfinished emotional business that somehow impacts their current relationships. Even if you're not aware of yours, it's there. Past experiences drive you at least part of the time.

If you're thinking "Not me" or just decided you have something more pressing to do than read on, you're resisting the idea that you have unresolved issues. That's fine; it just means the timing isn't right for you to explore this territory.

Eventually, you may get to the point where the past percolates up. A variety of life events can signal this transition—another separation or divorce, a child who's in serious trouble, a job loss, a traumatic event related to drugs or alcohol. Whatever it is, something tells you that you'd profit from taking an honest look at your life and relationships.

Remarried adults often become aware of repeating relationship patterns and wonder why they're occurring.

I thought everything would be different with Rick. He's not at all like my first husband. For several months, things were very new and exciting, and I was thrilled.

Then, some of the old feelings I'd had while married to my first husband started to come up. I started feeling resentful. I can't even remember what prompted these feelings now, but I vividly recall what they felt like.

I also remember what I thought. Whoa! I'd put myself and my children through the trauma of divorce because I'd been so unhappily married. Now the very same thing seemed to be starting all over again.

When it happened the first time—in my first marriage—I thought it was about him being a terrible partner. When it happened the second time, and with someone I loved so deeply, I began to wonder what was inside me that made me feel that way in a committed relationship.

(JULIE, FORTY-ONE, STEPCOUPLING FOR FOUR YEARS)

If your life hasn't yet provided the clues about where your unfinished emotional business lies and the idea intrigues you, here are some questions to help you begin to explore this topic.

- When do you feel most insecure or hurt in your relationship? Have you felt this way before? When? Do you remember feeling this way as a child?
- When are you most anxious? Have you felt this way before? When? With whom? As a child?

- When are you most angry? What provokes you? How do you express your anger? Do you lose your temper? Physically threaten or hurt people? Verbally abuse, degrade, or humiliate them? Withdraw? Who do you resemble when you're angry?
- In your relationship, when do you feel like a child— weak, insecure, incapable, powerless?

As you become aware of the situations that stimulate your feelings of hurt, fear, or anger, consider paying a different kind of attention when they arise. When you have a strong emotional reaction, you can either allow those emotions to run—tears, angry words, withdrawal, lashing out—or you can watch yourself run them. The first option maintains the status quo, the second allows for some growth. Much easier said than done, this requires you to take a step back from your experience.

One of the many situations in my first marriage that I resented was that my husband didn't do much around the house. Unless I asked him specifically to do something and then kept after him until it was done, I had to take care of everything.

One day I noticed that the carpet in the bedroom my second husband and I share needed to be vacuumed. Immediately, I felt the old, familiar fire of resentment even though, in my mind, I know that Scott does his fair share of stuff around the house.

While I vacuumed, feeling angry, I watched myself doing it. That was a shift. I was simultaneously angry and conscious of wondering, "What is this about?" It just couldn't be about Scott not doing enough.

(NANCY, THIRTY-FOUR, STEPCOUPLING FOR TWO YEARS)

When you have enough awareness about your response to observe it, you can consider talking about it. Doing so requires that you take the risk of sharing how you really feel with your partner.

He came in the room a few moments later and started to talk to me. In the past, I would have just been irritable. This time, even though it scared me, I told him that I was angry. I also explained to him that, in my first marriage, I had to do all the household stuff all the time and I really hated it. I felt like such a fool talking to him about this. To his everlasting credit, he just listened. He didn't take it personally. He listened carefully and then said, "Hmmm."

(NANCY, THIRTY-FOUR, STEPCOUPLING FOR TWO YEARS)

As you begin to understand that part of your emotional response arises from the past, you may be tempted to try to suppress your emotions, to choke back anger or blink back tears. Don't. The reason they still trouble you is because they haven't been adequately expressed and addressed. However, expression is different from acting out. "I'm so *angry*" is expressing your feelings. Raging and throwing things is acting out.

While expressing your feelings has the potential to rock your stepcouple boat, acting them out does more damage.

Later on, Scott and I talked about it. I thought he'd be upset that I was angry with him. He said that he'd much rather hear what was going on than to have me just be furious. We made love that night and that was different, too. Usually, if we fight, it takes at least a couple of days for us to want to be close to each other.

(NANCY, THIRTY-FOUR, STEPCOUPLING FOR TWO YEARS)

However, don't expect perfection from yourself. Even step-couples with a fair mastery of relationship skills still act out.

> *We do a pretty good job now most of the time. We've gotten to know each other's hot spots and how to respond. Every once in a while, though, one of us will still go ballistic. It can still get really ugly really fast. The only thing we can do at that point is to try to just stop because we're not fighting about what we think we're fighting about.*
>
> (NANCY, THIRTY-FOUR, STEPCOUPLING FOR TWO YEARS)

Here's a tried-and-true strategy for mending things—*Apologize!* If you have reason to believe that your behavior did or could have hurt your partner, you need to apologize. The power of a sincere apology to mend a dented relationship is immense. Apologizing gives you the opportunity to get out of your reaction and into your partner's perspective.

> *We had to literally agree on what constituted an apology. Before, we'd just kind of mumble "Sorry," if that.*
>
> *We agreed that, for us, an apology includes specifically mentioning the behavior we'd like to take back. If we can, we also try to explain what inside us prompted it. It's really important to both of us that the reason we give is about us, not the other person.*
>
> *For instance, I could say that I was sorry I got so angry about vacuuming. I might say that, because of my first marriage, it was hard for me to trust that I could count on him.*
>
> *What I wouldn't say is that I was angry because of something he did. Blaming him is worse than not apologizing.*
>
> (NANCY, THIRTY-FOUR, STEPCOUPLING FOR TWO YEARS)

When your unresolved emotional issues come to the surface, your partner isn't responsible for changing things so that you don't feel uncomfortable, angry or hurt. No matter how much he or she loves you and wants you to be happy, your mate can't take away your past or the reactions you have to it.

Exploring the ongoing effects of your past on your present life is obviously no mean feat. Yet it's critical to the success of your stepcouple and stepfamily.

For some people, the prospect of exploring past experiences involving hurt and loss is so threatening that they never embrace it. Their emotional lives often hold a string of failed relationships. They leave a trail of people behind them with whom once-close bonds have been replaced by anger, rage, resentment, hostility, hurt, or alienation.

The choice is yours. You can allow your unfinished business to run your life. Or you can plumb your past for the keys to your stepcouple's future.

We'd have a perfect relationship if it weren't for my thirteen-year-old stepson. He's the only reason we fight.

Stepcouples often identify a child as the primary source of their conflict. Trouble seems to start when the young agitator—the only child in the household or one of several—comes on the scene.

After we married, my wife and I fought mostly about her son. His behavior was out of line. He'd talk on the phone, play video games, never pick up his room. I viewed him as terribly undisciplined for a boy of thirteen. I wanted to shape him up.

> *I yelled at him frequently. My wife got upset with me for picking on him; I was too stern, she said. I thought she babied him, encouraging his sloppy ways.*
>
> *We got very, very angry with each other, just over him. We rarely fought about anything else.*
>
> (STEPDAD V, FORTY-SIX, STEPCOUPLING FOR TWO YEARS)

As I've mentioned before, children's emotions and behaviors can stress a stepcouple. Frequently, though, a seemingly incorrigible child signals a distressed adult or a troubled stepcouple relationship. When a child triggers or is the focus of adult fights, consider the possibility that the tension in your stepcouple is not about the child.

It's hazardous to rely on obvious explanations. The easy explanation for heartburn is spicy food, but a heart attack can also feel like indigestion. If you fail to understand the true nature of the situation, unpleasant or calamitous results can occur. Extending the practice of looking beyond surface appearances to your stepcouple and stepfamily is invaluable.

> *My older sister came to town on business and had dinner at the house. When I walked her to her car, she asked if I always rode my stepson so hard. I don't remember what I answered, but I didn't forget the question.*
>
> *My wife would think I was too stern because he's her child. My sister, that's different. Maybe there was something to it.*
>
> (STEPDAD V, FORTY-SIX, STEPCOUPLING FOR TWO YEARS)

Stepcouple and stepfamily tension isn't caused by just one person, adult or child. The irony about unfinished emotional business is this: The more sure you are that the problem lies with someone else, the more you can count on the fact that you, too, are contributing to the tension.

At this point, all you have to do is consider the possibility that you might be contributing to the conflict. Simply consider how your viewpoint, behavior, or response might fan the flames.

You may not like the idea. Loosening your grip on your point of view can seem stupid, crazy, pointless, or weak. If you've been convinced that changing someone else's behavior would solve your problem, deciding to consider what part *you* play in it can feel like you're giving in.

Think of it as getting over, instead. You're ready to get over responding the same way and expecting something new to happen. You're willing to rethink the head-spinning, heart-sinking need for another fierce fight over the same old stuff. Even better, you're ready to channel the energy you've used for fighting toward more productive, constructive purposes—for yourself, your stepcouple, and stepfamily.

One partner in a stepcouple can't induce this kind of willingness in the other partner with ultimatums, nagging, pleas, or any other ploy. You can only open one mind—yours.

> *Frankly, I was tired of the war at home. My wife and stepson weren't changing, nor was I. My sister's remark pointed me in a new direction.*
>
> *Before, I thought the only solution was for the boy to change. But my wife and I started seeing a counselor together to see if there were other answers.*
>
> (STEPDAD V, FORTY-SIX, STEPCOUPLING FOR TWO YEARS)

When you're ready to consider that more dynamics might be at work, you begin to have new ideas and experiences. You uncover new information or gain a fresh understanding of old facts.

> *One of the first things the counselor did was to ask my wife and me about our childhoods. Who raised us? What did they expect from us? How were we disciplined? And so forth.*
>
> *When it was my turn, I mentioned that both my grandfather and father had been marines. My grandfather had been a gunnery sergeant; my father was a pilot.*
>
> *As a child, I admired my father's courage and power. I also feared him. He ran our home with an iron fist. Every fall, he gave me a weekly schedule that included school, extracurricular activities, study time, and time to do my chores. I had to follow it, or I was punished.*
>
> *No wonder my stepson's free schedule irritated me so much.*
> (STEPDAD V, FORTY-SIX, STEPCOUPLING FOR TWO YEARS)

Until the issues originating in your past become clear, you tend to replicate the situation or situations that caused them. You'll find yourself drawn to people who fit key roles in the script you unconsciously wrote as a result of your previous experiences.

> *My parents never argued about how my father treated me, but it seemed to me that my mother thought he was too strict. She took no part in scheduling my life. She'd remind me, before he came home, to take care of something that would upset him. She protected me from his strictness as best she could.*
>
> *My wife, too, is a protective mother.*
> (STEPDAD V, FORTY-SIX, STEPCOUPLING FOR TWO YEARS)

Many people find that some aspect of their lives closely approximates a painful circumstance from childhood or a previous relationship. A woman whose father was a workaholic and whose first husband left her may be attracted to another emotionally unavailable man. A man whose mother died when he was a child may experience a string of relationships in which he feels abandoned. A woman whose parents fought bitterly may seek volatile mates.

Becoming aware of the congruence between the past and the present doesn't eliminate all conflict. It simply brings to your consciousness the connections that you were previously playing out unaware. The emotional power of the past no longer clings to your experience of the present.

> *I watched my stepson in a new way. I noticed that he did some things that were just normal for a boy his age. His friends did them, too. Of course, my wife had been telling me this for a long time.*
>
> *I still believe that he could be more disciplined, but I no longer feel so angry. I speak to him calmly now about cleaning up after himself and doing chores around the house.*
>
> (STEPDAD V, FORTY-SIX, STEPCOUPLING FOR TWO YEARS)

This stepfather released some of the controlling power he held when he no longer needed to micromanage his stepson's behavior. He empowered his wife and his stepson. But that's not what he notices the most.

> *I always had a knot of anger in my stomach around my stepson. I didn't know how tense I was until I relaxed around him a little.*
>
> (STEPDAD V, FORTY-SIX, STEPCOUPLING FOR TWO YEARS)

In the beginning, it feels like you lose power and position when you consider the possibility that you contribute to the conflict in your stepfamily. In reality, you gain perspective and a measure of peace.

My wife is really jealous of the time I spend with my son. When he's here for the weekend she barely speaks to me, and if he does anything wrong, she explodes. She says she wouldn't yell if I didn't ignore her when he's here, but I'm not ignoring her.

Remember, everyone has unfinished business. At any given time, either partner's response can be based on unresolved emotional issues. If your mate unknowingly acts out an episode from the past, rest assured that you'll eventually do so, too. Your response to your spouse's pain helps set the tenor of your relationship. Want to be understood and supported when your own stuff inevitably comes up? Set out to understand and support your partner.

You'll need awareness and patience. One partner with unfinished business stimulated by a particular situation often blames the experience on the other. The unspoken message is "It's *your* fault. If you would only behave differently, I wouldn't have to act this way."

Your mate may seem to give you the power to determine his or her response, becoming a passive victim of your behavior. So, on the one hand, it can feel like your mate willingly hands all the power in your relationship to you.

However, the reverse is actually true. Because your partner's angry, blaming response arises partially or completely from past hurt and loss, you have limited power to change his or her experience. If the issue existed only in the present, you could

make needed amends and move on. You can't undo your partner's past, though, no matter how loving and attentive you are.
That's why you may feel as though nothing you do satisfies
your mate.

Set an alternative goal. You *can* set the stage for your partner
to understand him or herself better and to take charge again of
his or her experience. Successful stepcouples learn to do this.
The key is to avoid, as much as you can, participating in the
play of the past.

When your partner rages or acts out in other inappropriate
ways, clearly and calmly convey that your relationship deserves
better. If you can deliver this message lovingly, so much the
better. Try very hard not to take your partner's intense emotions personally.

*I had your garden-variety terrible childhood. My mother raged
constantly, and I lived in terror. Not surprisingly, when I grew
up, I also exploded at the drop of a hat.*

*The first few times I screamed after we got together, Ted
said, "We're not going there." That was it. He didn't get mad
at me or walk out. He just made it very clear that I had to find
another way of expressing my feelings if I wanted to be around
him. No one had ever treated my anger that calmly before,
especially no one who was close to me.*

(MARGARET, FORTY-SIX, STEPCOUPLING
FOR EIGHT YEARS)

The best and most challenging response to a reactive partner is to keep your own emotions in check. Remember the
importance of defusing the situation with a time out or other
similar strategy. Many stepcouples set up these ground rules
ahead of time.

Ted and I agree to use time outs. If we notice that either one of us is becoming too upset, we take fifteen minutes out to calm down. In theory, this is a nice, tidy plan.

What sometimes happens is that I have a hard time stopping. Ted'll say "Time out" and I'll want to say one last thing. He doesn't take the bait, though, which can further infuriate me. By the time I actually stop, I need more like an hour or two to calm down.

I'm working on stopping sooner.

(MARGARET, FORTY-SIX, STEPCOUPLING
FOR EIGHT YEARS)

When unfinished business emerges, you symbolize someone from your partner's past: a parent, previous spouse, or other significant individual. You and your predecessor temporarily occupy the same space in your partner's emotional life. When your partner demands that you provide enough attention or affection to keep him or her from feeling angry or hurt, remember that you're being asked to heal wounds you didn't create. Resist the temptation to jump into the box your mate built for you.

Acknowledge his or her feelings of hurt, loss, or anger. Ask for a few specific behaviors he or she would like you to drop or adopt. If you can comfortably and realistically commit to them, do so. For example, giving regular, reassuring hugs during a child's visitation weekend is realistic.

On the other hand, changing your child's visitation schedule so your partner doesn't have to share you is not realistic. When your mate requests something you can't provide, say so as lovingly as you can. "I'm sorry that you're hurting. I'm here for you, but I can't give you that." A calm and supportive delivery conveys the message that you care about your partner and are committed to your relationship, even though you don't like the behavior.

> *Bill was infinitely patient with me when we first married. I was a mess, furious with his kids, furious with him for being gone so much at work. I can't remember him ever lashing out at me, although it must have been very difficult.*
>
> (SHARON, FIFTY-SIX, STEPCOUPLING
> FOR TWENTY-EIGHT YEARS)

The more you convey love for and commitment to your partner, without being drawn into his or her emotional issue, the better the odds that he or she can take the next step: self-examination.

To lessen the impact of unresolved emotional issues, your partner must be willing to explore their roots and effects. He or she needs a detached curiosity about the experience to begin to understand how the past influences the present.

Your partner has to reach this point freely. Your support and love make it easier, but you can't dictate the timing or even the eventual occurrence of self-awareness and willingness.

> *Maybe once or twice, Bill very tactfully suggested that I was making things harder than they needed to be, that I seemed to be struggling with something other than just raising children. I'm sure I wasn't happy to hear that.*
>
> (SHARON, FIFTY-SIX, STEPCOUPLING
> FOR TWENTY-EIGHT YEARS)

Over time, as your partner feels safe in and grows confident about your stepcouple, he or she begins to look at the links between the present and the past.

Finally, finally, after what seemed like a very long time, I began to understand that I was part of the problem. I was trying very hard to be perfect because I was afraid of losing Bill the way I'd lost my first husband. I had to be the perfect stepmother, the perfect wife. Have perfect children, et cetera.

The pressure I put on myself was driving me crazy, and I took it out on him.

(SHARON, FIFTY-SIX, STEPCOUPLING
FOR TWENTY-EIGHT YEARS)

Time together also offers a stepcouple the experience of knowing how your partner expresses his or her unfinished emotional business. You begin to understand what triggers it, how it appears and develops, how long it tends to last, how intense it is and, most important, how best to support your mate without being drawn into the drama. This information empowers you.

You also have the power of love. You chose your mate because you wanted to spend the rest of your lives together. In order to do that, you need the strength and courage to embrace the paths that converged when you met.

We've been seeing a marriage counselor for several months. He's suggested a number of things that we could do differently. They help for a little while, then we go right back to fighting about the same things we always fight about.

When unresolved emotional issues cause tension in your stepcouple relationship, simply changing behaviors doesn't fix the underlying problem. There are some basic changes that oil the gears of exploring unfinished emotional business: not taking things personally, watching yourself react instead of doing so unconsciously, remembering to apologize when appropriate. Undertake these changes as a means, not an end. Over time, as you understand the motivation for your actions and responses, you'll be able to make significant changes that stick.

> *We tried many things to resolve our differences about money. Nearly every month, we'd come up with a new way of paying bills, combining money, handling household expenses. Nothing stuck.*
>
> *Only when we stopped talking about how to handle money and started talking about how we felt did we begin to make some progress. We decided to find a counselor to help us move things along.*
>
> (NANCY, THIRTY-FOUR, STEPCOUPLING FOR TWO YEARS)

Individual counseling can accelerate the process of understanding yourself better. For a stepcouple, an objective third person who's familiar with the unique dynamics of stepfamilies can provide a lifeline when the two of you drift in a current of intense emotions.

Counseling, however, is no panacea. When you're dragging a reluctant partner along for couples therapy, are not emotionally ready to try therapy, or are seeing the wrong counseling professional, you're unlikely to profit much from the experience. Make sure you know when to pursue it, what to look for, and what you can expect from effective counseling.

When might you consider seeking counseling? One of the best reasons is if you want to increase and improve the intimacy in your stepcouple relationship, but you're stymied about how to go about it. If you've noticed a repeating pattern in your relationships, a good counseling relationship can help you explore the dynamics involved. Curiosity about yourself and your stepcouple relationship, rather than judgment, is a good starting point for a deeper look.

To find a counseling relationship that works, identify some basic criteria: gender, location, educational background if it matters to you, fees, and so forth. Gather the names of some possible counselors by asking friends and others whose opinions you trust to recommend someone.

> *We went to see a woman who was very highly recommended by a number of people. They all just loved her. I felt tense from almost the moment I walked in the door. I didn't like her. We didn't even make another appointment.*
>
> *As soon as we met the next woman on our list, we both knew it was the right place for us to be.*
>
> (NANCY, THIRTY-FOUR, STEPCOUPLING FOR TWO YEARS)

An effective counseling relationship can provide the support that allows you to address your issues. You can receive mentoring about new ways of being in a relationship and help in setting realistic goals within a framework that holds you accountable for your choices. In truth, any healthy relationship with a friend, mate, or relative who allows you to safely express your feelings and thoughts and offers a modicum of wisdom can provide these things for you. One of the benefits of cultivating a relationship with a counselor, though, is that you get unbiased professional expertise.

With safe support, you can revisit relationships and experiences with the intention of bringing them into the open. Your experience of revisiting these events and memories rarely lives up to your fear about what you'll find. Bringing the memories and their accompanying feelings and thoughts into the open allows you to disconnect them from your present experience.

With the help of our counselor, we started to work backward from our current experiences about money and in our relationship to what they reminded us of. We realized that we both had big hurts in our backgrounds.

I didn't believe I could ever trust a man. I learned this from my mom. My dad gambled. She didn't trust him and, while I was growing up, she told stories about how he wasted money. When my mate didn't do exactly what I expected about money, I felt like my worst fears were coming true. I was being betrayed.

His mom died when he was a kid. If I acted financially independent, he felt I didn't need him and would eventually leave.

Until we realized these things, we thought we were fighting about money. It wasn't about money at all. It was about our fears of being betrayed or abandoned.

(NANCY, THIRTY-FOUR, STEPCOUPLING FOR TWO YEARS)

When you disconnect the power of history from the present by understanding your past emotional experiences, you become more free to choose your present response. Even though you may still feel some of the same feelings, you can handle them differently.

Money still isn't a very comfortable topic for us, but it's not out of control anymore. I can remind myself that part of the reason it's hard has nothing to do with now.

I understand him and his insecurities better now, too. It's like before I only saw what I feared. I do appreciate him and all the things he does, and I'm working on trusting.

It's not perfect, but it's a whole lot better.

(NANCY, THIRTY-FOUR, STEPCOUPLING FOR TWO YEARS)

"Better" is a realistic goal of exploring unresolved emotional issues. Core emotional fears—of abandonment, betrayal, or loss, that you're not good enough, that you won't ever have enough—emerge over and over for the duration of your life. As you understand how these fears play out in your present, their impact gradually lessens, but they never completely resolve. You'll always be tempted, at least a little, to succumb to them.

Many people notice that their unresolved emotional issues surface in cycles. Certain stressors may always stimulate your fears. Particularly as you become more secure in your stepcouple relationship and more familiar with each other, you can go months without experiencing their effects. Your issues are still there, however, and will inevitably be triggered somewhere down the line.

Any relationship that's supportive in a healthy way, including counseling, can help you befriend these aspects of yourself. Far from being some kind of defect to be eradicated, your lifelong emotional Achilles heel is part and parcel of who you are. Your mate's core issues are equally integral to his or her personality.

Successful stepcouples know this. Both partners actively applaud each other's strengths and accomplishments and gently shore each other up when they falter, knowing that love encompasses all that each individual brings to the union.

eight

Looking Back:
One Stepcouple's Story

Bill and Sharon fell blindly in love twenty-nine years ago. Both were raising their children alone, having been left by their former spouses who then moved out of the area.

Sharon says, "The first night we went out, I just knew. The first time he picked me up, he had one of my favorite tapes on his car stereo. He's funny and smart, and I was crazy about him." Bill says, "I found her very attractive—still do. She's easy to talk to, interested in other people. I liked it that she had a fulfilling life of her own, too."

After dating for a few weeks, they widened their infatuated focus on each other and planned an afternoon hike with their children. "Part of me wanted to forget the kids and just be with Bill, and part of me thought we should do something with the kids," says Sharon. "The part that thought we should include the kids won."

They packed two adults and four kids into Bill's car. "My daughter said 'Do we *have* to?'" remembers Bill. "She knew Sharon's boys slightly from school, so it wasn't the case that she objected to them. At thirteen, she just wanted to do her own thing."

Sharon's boys were the youngest of the four children at seven and nine, and the most enthusiastic—at least initially. A few minutes into the forty-five-minute hike, their boisterous energy gave way to grumbling. "We imagined such a different afternoon," says Sharon. "My boys started right away with 'Are we there yet? This is *boring*.' Then the youngest just plopped down

231

on the trail, saying he needed a rest. Getting them to go along was like hauling a load up a hill."

Things didn't improve after the hike, either. Bill and Sharon took the children out for an early dinner at a family restaurant.

Raised in a formal family, Bill expected certain behavior from children. "Her kids were hellions. They had no manners. They couldn't sit still for more than a few minutes and fought with each other at the table. Finally, she told them to go out and play in the parking lot.

"I thought 'This is going to be trouble,'" says Bill. "We clearly had big differences in parenting."

Sharon's thoughts ran along different lines. "I figured I'd never see him again," she says. "I thought, 'He's a very nice man and he'll never call me again.'"

He called. They became engaged a year later.

"My immediate response when we decided to get married was delight that I'd have more children," says Sharon. "I was fond of Bill's kids; they were nice and well-mannered. I figured I'd just move into mothering them. I'd get to do girl stuff because now I'd have a daughter."

Bill recalls that his children seemed pleased about the wedding. "They both got new clothes, she got to wear flowers, they got to participate in the ceremony. They thought that was cool." However, if there was a fly in the ointment during their engagement, it was his daughter. Just entering her teen years, she focused more on her friends than family activities. Sharon felt some resistance from her stepdaughter about having a new mother; certainly, Gina didn't want another adult telling her what to do.

Sharon's biological sons were also excited about their marriage. "It meant they got to live in Bill's house, which they thought was so cool."

And live in Bill's house they did. Both Bill and Sharon had sole custody of their children. They spent their wedding night at a downtown hotel alone, had a gourmet brunch, and then went home to their brood.

The honeymoon phase of their stepcouple lasted only a month or two. "Right after the wedding, it was, Let the adjustment begin!" says Sharon. "I was immediately plunged into kid stuff, home all the time with the four kids. Bill was very busy at work. Because we had all four children all the time, we got away only on date nights and when we occasionally traveled on business.

"My plans to mother his kids didn't pan out because they missed their biological mother terribly. They saw little of her and they couldn't sort it out. They weren't very trusting of women. They also loved their dad a whole lot and resented somebody moving in on their relationship with him. They wanted me out; they wanted their dad to themselves."

Bill and Sharon's children showed definite signs of trouble adjusting to the changes in their lives. Their grades plummeted, and phone calls from school about behavior problems became frequent. As the children moved into their teen years, their acting out grew increasingly troublesome.

"There were good times, too," says Sharon. "We went camping and skied together as a family. Graduations, band concerts, soccer games. There were things to cheer about.

"But, frankly, the first few years are a blur. Bill felt a lot of pressure to produce at work to provide money for the family. I was pulling on him, saying, 'Get yourself home because these kids are driving me crazy.'

"I don't think Bill's children fantasized about their parents reconciling and being a happy couple again. I think it was clear to them that their parents' marriage was over. But they definitely missed their mom. And they didn't want *me;* they were going to get me out. They were mean and ugly and awful and disobedient. I have to admit, I was mean and ugly right back. I'm not proud of some of the things I said and did.

"It was very, very hard on our marriage. There were many times when I was outraged at something one of his kids had done or said. And I was very angry at him for having such terrible kids and not making them behave better. He'd come home from work and I'd jump all over him. He would say, 'OK, honey' and he'd talk to them very calmly when I thought he should be reading them the riot act."

Bill seconds these memories. "It was frustrating. After a long day at the office, I'd listen to her and then have to cope. I'd go deal with the kid, but only because Sharon asked me to. I often didn't even understand what the problem was that I was supposed to be fixing.

"Her boys and I had a little easier relationship. I knew they missed their father terribly, and I decided early on that, rather than replace him, I was going to be more like a kindly uncle. They were careful around me and a little distant. That distance could have been a two-way street."

Sharon continues, "I don't think of those years as being pleasant for the kids. There were lots of demands and lots of fights. The adults in their lives had made earthshaking changes, and the children had no say in how anything turned out. Because they all saw so little of their other parents, we got the brunt of their anger and sadness. It was grueling for three or four years."

One day Sharon reached the bottom. Desperate and upset, she felt at the end of her rope. "I had no plan, nowhere to go, no family or friends whose house I could move into. I didn't have an apartment lined up. I didn't know what I was going to do. I just knew that it wasn't working."

Looking back, Sharon has some perspective on the conversation with her stepdaughter, Gina, that followed. "Things had been bad between us and getting worse. She wouldn't mind me. I'd threaten her and then not follow through. I had no idea how to get her to behave. Finally, I just told her that I'd done everything I could do as a stepmother. I couldn't keep on going the way we'd been. I had nothing else left to try. I was upset, hurt, and angry, and she saw that.

"It was the first time I set a firm boundary with her. And it was the first time I expressed my feelings authentically. I didn't rage at her. I just told her that I was almost used up.

"She later said that it shook her up, to know that I had limits. Her behavior shifted a modicum. Around the same time, and it took far longer than I would have expected, the children began to get over some of their anger. As time kept passing, the reality of their lives began to sink in. We began to settle in as a family. They became more interested in other things—school and sports. They began to feel more connected with the way we did things as a family."

What kept them together during those difficult years? Sharon says she and her husband have something she believes will always keep them together. "First of all, we were a really strong couple, and we used our relationship pretty well. Neither one of us tried to sabotage the other. Of course, occasionally one or the other of us would think 'This is a bad deal for me and my kids.' But we were such a strong couple that we tried hard to understand and support each other. Even during the bad times."

Bill adds, "I always knew we were devoted to each other. There were one or two times when I thought, 'Why did I do this to myself?' On the worst days, I had an overview that the kids would eventually grow up and leave home."

They agree that date nights and placing a priority on their stepcouple in other ways helped their marriage endure. Bill says, "Our kids would probably say that we were such a strong couple that we sometimes neglected them. In reality, we were both 'on' all the time. We didn't have the back and forth of visitation, so we didn't get much relief from herding kids. It was exhausting, and we had to pay attention to each other to get through it."

Sharon relates another pivotal moment in her experience as a stepmother. "For a long time, I prayed for something or someone to rescue me. It never happened. At some point, I began to deeply believe that my family was all of us, not just Bill and me. I realized that it would never be just the two of us, at least not until the children grew up and moved out.

"Around the same time, I changed from thinking 'I'm going to be my stepchildren's perfect mother' to acknowledging that they had history and genes that I wasn't a part of. Before that, I went back and forth between wanting too little and then way too much of these kids.

"I was their stepmom, married to their dad, and I was responsible for their daily routines and activities because I ran the household. I was 'Mom' only to my own kids. My stepkids already had a mom they loved. That's the reality, the way it was. When I accepted reality, I didn't have to be the perfect stepmother anymore. I stopped living in a fantasy world, waiting to get rescued, too."

Sharon smiles as she continues, "That's kind of a neat experience to know that no one's going to rescue you. You have to step up to the plate. And when you do, you find out how much you're capable of. That's empowering."

"I think that it was a gift for me to grow and expand and stretch and do things I had no clue about or didn't think I could do. Kids, especially stepkids, push you. You have two ways to go: be there for them or get out. You've got to do your job. If I had never married Bill and been part of a stepfamily, I don't think I'd be as strong as I am now. Strength, confidence, and competence—that's what I've gained."

Bill adds, "When we look back, raising each other's children was the most difficult thing. Our children had problems and so did we, raising them."

Sharon adds, "We also had some resentment toward our ex-spouses. They got off scot-free and we did all the work. I resented his ex-wife for having her children and then leaving. Bill resented my ex-spouse who only partially financially supported my children.

"It was also hard that we felt so alone as a couple. There was not much information about stepfamilies out there. People just didn't talk about it. I guess there were a couple of books, but I didn't read them. We made a second marriage and a stepfamily by guess and by golly. I think there was a support group in the area, but I don't remember that I ever went. We were doing it alone.

"None of our friends were stepcouples. That was one of the hardest parts, because I felt such a weird aloneness, knowing that nobody understood what I was feeling. I felt ostracized and isolated because my friends only had their biological children to care for. They weren't raising someone else's children the way I was.

"As I said, I contemplated leaving sometimes. But when I thought about what I'd give up, there's no way that I would have ever left. The other thing I stayed for is the kids; I thought they needed stability and parents who were going to be there for them. They needed and deserved to have a family, for God's sakes. I'm the one who signed up, and I wasn't going to give up."

Sharon lays a piece of ruled school paper on the table. Here's what it says:

Dear Sharon,

I found myself thinking about you and how you've played a part in my life.

I can't remember if I've ever shown you any appreciation for raising me. I guess I've left that up to your intuition. However, it probably wouldn't hurt if I sent a little thanks your way. At least, I hope not.

I think back in my life, and it occurs to me that you are the most consistent figure in my growing up. Consistency is important to me. You were there. You didn't run away. However, I'm sorry I didn't take advantage of it. I guess I didn't trust anyone enough to let them close to me.

Anyway, it's your model of consistency that I'm building off of now. I'm not saying I agreed with or liked the way you reacted to every situation, but you were consistently there to deal with everything with the same caring.

I don't mean for this letter to conjure up ill feelings of my childhood or for you to bear that burden. I hoped it would free you of any feeling of failure. You didn't fail. You did a hell of a job even with the bad stuff we threw in your face. You never gave up. Kind of like a pit bull with its jaws locked on its fiercest prey, and if there is any quality about myself that I can attribute to you, it is that.

Somewhere between your caring and consistency, my father's ability to rationally deal with things and my mother's imagination lies the person I try to be—in that order. I hope you share this letter with my father. There is so much of me that is like him and so much of him that I strive to be.

I hope your taking us all into your life didn't have too adverse an effect on you and your sons. I realize more and more how hard it must have been on them. Hopefully, this story will have a happier ending than its beginning.

Thanks.

Love,

Steve

"My stepson wrote this when he went away for a summer job," says Sharon. "I couldn't believe it when I got it in the mail. It seemed like we were at such odds for so long. I can't tell you how much his letter touched me.

"Over time there's been such healing for all of us. After twenty-eight years, we're truly family. Although there are some sad and angry memories, there's no hostility, anger, or doubt now. For my part, I don't put my stepkids in one box and my own in another. I think the kids' only leftover is their memories of having to share: parents, money, food, space . . . all the stuff of daily life.

"All four kids think of us and call us 'their parents' and 'their family.' But when they're talking about us as individuals, they make—and rightfully so—a distinction between Mom or Dad and 'Sharon' or 'Bill.' They all already have a biological mom and dad they call Mom and Dad. To them, we're 'Mom and Bill' or 'Dad and Sharon.' My sons would never introduce Bill as their father, even though they're very fond of him. Even twenty-eight years later, our kids use those words: 'stepmom,' 'stepdad.' There's no shame in that."

Three of Sharon and Bill's children are now married and starting families of their own. All three weddings were such a wonderful celebration for our kids. Our exes and their spouses were present and very involved in the events.

"In fact, my son asked me to walk him down the aisle. Right behind us were my two husbands, his biological father and stepfather. It was a proud and happy moment. At the reception, Fred, my first husband, read a toast that he had prepared. He thanked me for being the mother to his children. He thanked Bill and me both and recognized the patience and guidance it took to lead his children, through the ups and downs of adolescence. He thanked Bill for being there for his son. It took our breath away for a minute.

"Now we have four grandchildren. I remember when my stepdaughter told us she was pregnant. We were in Mexico, the first family vacation in years. My birthday happened to fall during that trip. That evening, we gathered together. The kids all gave me wonderful gifts; my stepson wrote me a poem." Sharon's eyes fill with tears for the first time. "Gina said she had something to tell us, that we were all going to be grandparents and aunts and uncles. I remember how I felt, how thrilled! Of course, I cried. What a great birthday gift!

"Bill's ex-wife lives out of town, but she visits her kids and grandchildren frequently. She came in for one of the grandchildren's birthdays. The two of us sat on the couch together and chewed the fat. She told me stories of what Gina had been like as a small child and how much her granddaughter reminds her of Gina as a baby.

"How things have changed. I used to be so jealous of Bill's first wife. I can remember hearing stories about her romance with Bill. In their early family photos, he's with her and their children. He loved her, he says he did. I wanted to be number one—don't we all?—and I was also angry that he had two kids with her. I don't know where all those negative feelings went, but they're gone now.

"They feel like ancient history now. I'll admit, some of the last twenty-eight years is a blur. I'm really proud of our whole family. They're wonderful adults. My older son married a woman with a son, so he's a stepdad. He and his wife are raising her boy together. So we're step-stepgrandparents, too, if that's what you'd call it." Sharon's tears are long gone, replaced once again by her smile.

"One of the things we're thinking about now is retirement and wills and estate planning. How can we make sure that all the children are treated equitably? Stepstuff never stops. Also, our children have two sets of parents that they have to worry about.

"Those are the kinds of issues that come up for us now. I'm sure we'll find solutions that work for our family. We've come so far."

About two years ago, Sharon's younger son and his then-fiancée called her and asked if she'd like to go on a short hike with them. Sharon recalls the afternoon. "We took the same walk we'd taken so many years ago, the one Bill and I first took all those kids on. It's my favorite walk."

The experience jogged her memory. She asked her son if he recalled that first outing. He was seven years old at the time.

He couldn't remember a thing.

"You were horrible," Sharon reminded him. "You were such a brat."

"I probably was," he replied. Acknowledging the number of years that had passed, Sharon and her son marked the moment and moved on.

Sharon and Bill—and all enduring stepcouples—know about moving on. They've embraced impermanence. Successful stepcouples emerge when adults move beyond one marriage, one form of family, one set of hopes and dreams to another. Enduring stepcouples learn, too, to cultivate the art and skill of moving on, allowing the present to define itself, encumbered only by history worth carrying.

Appendix: Resources for Stepcouples

Organizations

Stepfamily Association of America

National Headquarters   650 J Street, Suite 205
                             Lincoln, NE 68508
                             (800) 735-0329

Alabama
  North Alabama   Judy Stalcup
                             Florence, AL 35630
                             (205) 766-6588
                             (205) 718-0804

  Central Alabama   Barry Bennett
                             Sumiton, AL 35148
                             (205) 648-3614
                             (205) 648-3488
                             bgd.ew@netzero.net

Arizona:
  Tuscon Chapter   Ren Jones
                             Tucson, AZ 85712
                             (520) 751-2847
                             (520) 320-5075

Arkansas
  Stepfamilies   Theresa Paxton
    of Arkansas   Fort Smith, AR 72904
                             (501) 783-2247

Step-Carefully   Bobby Collins
                      Fort Smith, AR 72917
                      (501) 410-1009
                      (501) 474-9102
                      step@stepcarefully.com

California
  Central Valley   Dava Ann Berlinger-Butler
                      Sacramento, CA 95828
                      (916) 681-3659

  Los Alamitos   Yaffia Balsam
                      Los Alamitos, CA 90720
                      (562) 598-2223

  Santa Ana   Vincent Redmond
                      Santa Ana, CA 92670
                      (714) 358-9831

  Solano Chapter   Ann Sheldon-Russell
    (Fairfield)   Fairfield, CA 94533
                      (707) 421-1069
                      (707) 421-1785

  Contra Costa   Karin Scholdberg
                      Danville, CA 94526
                      (925) 838-2382

  Lompoc Valley   Bill Kissee
                      Lompoc, CA 93436
                      (805) 736-6415

  Oakland/East Bay   Anthony Carpentieri
                      Berkeley, CA 94609
                      (510) 653-6344

Silicon Valley	Susan English Los Gatos, CA 95030 (408) 395-1308
San Francisco	Frances Verrinder San Francisco, CA 94131 (415) 550-0677 (415) 647-3262
Peninsula/San Jose	Bob and Stacy Matthews San Jose, CA 95101 (408) 225-9409
Santa Cruz	Gail Davis Santa Cruz, CA 95062 (831) 426-7322 (831) 427-4510
Redwood Empire	Karen Peterson Santa Rosa, CA 95405 (707) 545-9444 (707) 541-7153
Marin Stepfamilies	Susan Pieper-Bailey Larkspur, CA 94941 (415) 892-5505 (415) 902-0852
San Diego North	Pam Laidlaw San Diego, CA 92130 (760) 755-1260 (760) 759-1359
La Mesa	Joyce Stone San Diego, CA 92109 (619) 699-3546

San Diego Central   Pam Badger
                    La Mesa, CA 91941
                    (619) 221-7866
                    (619) 759-2263

Colorado
  Grand Junction   Daphine Wissel
                    Grand Junction, CO 81501
                    (970) 245-1571

  Fort Collins   Steve Bunten
                    Fort Collins, CO 80525
                    (970) 225-1668

Connecticut
  Stepfamilies of   Elaine Formica
     Connecticut   Manchester, CT 06405
                    (860) 647-3330

Florida
  Broward County   Dr. Mitch Spero
                    Plantation, FL 33317
                    (954) 587-7520

  Big Bend   Mari Anne Guzman
                    Tallahassee, FL 32308
                    (850) 668-4068

Georgia
  North Atlanta   Sue Parnell
                    Roswell, GA 33075
                    (770) 594-0520

  New Beginnings   John Elliott
                    McDonough, GA 30253
                    (770) 957-3782
                    (770) 471-3633

Idaho
    Southwest Idaho   Marion Summers
                               Boise, ID 83704
                               (208) 376-3720

Illinois
    Illinois Chapter   Brenda Nemeth
                               Arlington Heights, IL 60004
                               (847) 255-6736
                               (815) 455-6736

Indiana
    Indiana Chapter   Margaret Ridderheim
                               Leo, IN 46765
                               (219) 627-6411

Iowa
    Central Iowa   Jim Johns
                               Runnells, IA 50237
                               (515) 964-9524

Louisiana
    South Louisiana   Suzanne Reveley
                               New Orleans, LA 70125
                               (504) 866-3477
                               (504) 896-9591

Maryland
    Baltimore   Neil and Debbie Zimmerman
                               Baltimore, MD 21236
                               (410) 529-7176
                               (410) 965-8294

    Montgomery   Amy Scott
                               Bethesda, MD 20906
                               (301) 656-3225

Howard County   Barbara Fowler
                    Columbia, MD 21045
                    (410) 381-2402

Massachussetts
   Central   Lynne Doody
   Massachusetts   Worcester, MA 01605
                    (508) 853-1409
                    (978) 464-5451

Michigan
   Washtenaw   Nick Meima, Allison Welles,
                    or Katheryn Sholder
                    Ann Arbor, MI 48103
                    (734) 663-5853
                    (734) 663-6204
                    (734) 764-5392

   Monroe   Denise Gleason
                    Monroe, MI 48162
                    (734) 241-2417

Missouri
   Gateway Chapter Bill Schermes
                    Valley Park, MO 63088
                    (314) 876-6868

Nebraska
   Lincoln   C. J. Johnson
   Stepfamilies   Lincoln, NE 68505
                    (402) 483-2431

New Hampshire
   Southern   Christine Landry-Terrasi
   New Hampshire   Salem, NH 03079
                    (603) 595-3522

New Jersey
North Jersey   Merry Mans
Westwood, NJ 07675
(201) 767-4571

South Jersey   Richard and Catherine Dudley
Cherry Hill, NJ 08034
(609) 321-0145
SNJStepFam@aol.com

Central   Caryl Tipton
Hamilton Square, NJ 08690
(609) 588-8779
(609) 695-0329 x 2224

New Mexico
Albuquerque   Kandace Blanchard
Chapter   Albuquerque, NM 87111
(505) 275-0000
(505) 345-9190

New York
Buffalo   Christopher Pino
Buffalo, NY 14214
(716) 832-1434

Brooklyn Chapter   Elizabeth Jacobs-Pinson
Brooklyn, NY 11213
(718) 773-9054
hapi@idtint

Metro New York   Helen Crohn
New York, NY 10019
(212) 632-4676

Rochester   Estalyn Walcoff
                          Rochester, NY 14618
                          (716) 442-3440

Ohio
   Northwest Ohio   Rene Hamilton
                          Toledo, OH 43560
                          (419) 693-6330
                          (419) 885-1910

Oklahoma
   Oklahoma City   Sherry Martin
                          Oklahoma City, OK 73112
                          (405) 848-8482

Oregon
   Central Oregon   Julieann Fouts
                          Bend, OR 97709
                          (541) 330-1382
                          (541) 317-8478

   Eugene   Allison Fountain
                          Eugene, OR 97401
                          (541) 344-3440

Pennsylvania
   Stepfamilies   Gloria Clark
      of Pittsburgh   Pittsburgh, PA 15206
                          (412) 361-6767

   Pittsburgh   Heather and Robert Trivus
      South Hills   Pittsburgh, PA 15228
                          (412) 343-1009
                          (412) 531-2520

Lehigh Valley   Joseph Maher or Deb Romberger
                       Allentown, PA 18103
                       (610) 791-3581
                       (610) 437-3612

Living in Step   Dawn Edwards
                       Warren, PA 16365
                       (814) 726-2319

Texas
Bay Area   Andria Varsos
                       Houston, TX 77062
                       (281) 486-9224

Greenway   Steve Katzman
   Stepfamilies   Houston, TX 77027
                       (713) 572-0222

Brazos Valley   Kelly Quinn
                       Bryan, TX 77808
                       (409) 774-1141
                       (409) 402-4766

SW Houston   Norma Valdez
                       Houston, TX 77081
                       (713) 660-8137

Virginia
North Virginia   DeeDee Pickett
                       Fairfax, VA 22030
                       (703) 352-9048

Washington
Olympia   Brian Kennedy
   Stepfamilies   Olympia, WA 98051
                       (206) 352-1668

Seattle Eastside	Loreen Miki–Bosler
Chapter	Kirkland, WA 98033
	(425) 985-3890

Wisconsin
Metro Milwaukee   Grant Anderson
                   Milwaukee, WI 53005

Canada
Durham   Carolyn Haugen
                   Port Perry, Ontario
                   (905) 985-1762

Websites

About.com
www.stepparenting.about.com

Divorce Source, Inc.
www.divorcesource.com

Divorcenet
www.divorcenet.com

ivillage, Parents Place.com
www.parentsplace.com/family/stepfamilies

Kids in the Middle
www.kidsinthemiddle.org

National Center for Fathering
www.fathers.com/articles

Parenting Today's Teen
www.parentingteens.com/stepfamarchive.html

Second Wives Club
www.secondwivesclub.com

Stepcoupling
www.stepcoupling.com

Stepdads.com
www.stepdads.com

Stepfamily Association of America
www.stepfam.org

Stepfamily Association of Illinois, Inc.
www.stepfamilyinfo.org

Stepfamily Consultation & Counseling
www.stepfamilyseattle.com

Stepfamily Foundation
www.stepfamily.org

Stepmothers International
www.stepmothers.org

The Stepfamily Connection
www.tsconnection.com

The Stepfamily Network, Inc.
www.stepfamily.net

The Stepmoms Network
www.stepmoms.net

women.com
www.womenswire.com/stepmoms

bibliography

Remarriage

Barash, Susan Shapiro. *Second Wives: The Pitfalls and Rewards of Marrying Widowers and Divorced Men.* Far Hills, N.J.: New Horizon Press, 2000.

Estess, Patricia Schiff. *Money Advice for Your Successful Remarriage: Handling Delicate Financial Issues with Love and Understanding.* Cincinnati, Ohio: Betterway Books, 1996.

Gottman, John, with Nancy Silver. *Why Marriages Succeed or Fail, and How You Can Make Yours Last.* New York: Simon and Schuster, 1994.

———. *The Seven Principles for Making Marriage Work.* New York: Three Rivers Press, 2000.

Hamburg, Samuel R. *Will Our Love Last? A Couple's Roadmap.* New York: Scribner's, 2000.

Millian, Lenore Fogelson, and Steven Jerry Millian. *The Second Wives Club: Secrets for Becoming Lovers for Life.* Hillsboro, Oreg.: Beyond Words, 1999

Moseley, Douglas, and Naomi Moseley. *Making Your Second Marriage a First Class Success.* Roseville, Calif.: Prima Publishing, 1998.

Sweet, Rose. *How to Be First in a Second Marriage: Healing and Forgiveness for All Concerned.* College Press, 1999.

Thomas, Christine. *Second Wives: The Silent Struggle.* Seattle, Wash.: Fender Publishing Co., 1999.

Wright, Norman H. *Before You Remarry.* Eugene, Oreg.: Harvest House, Inc., 1999.

Stepfamilies

Bray, James H., and John Kelly. *Stepfamilies: Love, Marriage & Parenting in the First Decade.* New York: Broadway Books, 1998.

Erwin, Cheryl, H. Stephen Glenn, and Jane Nelsen. *Positive Discipline for Your Stepfamily: Nurturing Harmony, Respect and Joy in Your New Family.* Roseville, Calif.: Prima Publishing, 2000.

Hurwitz, Jane. *Coping in a Blended Family.* New York: Rosen Publishing Co., 1997.

Lauer, Robert H., and Jeanette C. Lauer. *Becoming Family: How to Build a Stepfamily That Really Works.* Minneapolis, Minn.: Augsburg Fortress Publications, 1999.

Shimberg, Elaine Fantle. *Blending Families: A Guide for Parents, Stepparents and Everyone Building a Successful New Family.* Berkeley, Calif.: Berkeley Publishing Group, 1999.

Wallerstein, Judith, and Sandra Blakeslee (contributor). *Second Chances: Men, Women and Children a Decade After Divorce.* Boston: Houghton Mifflin Co., 1996.

Wallerstein, Judith, Julia M. Lewis, and Sandra Blakeslee. *The Unexpected Legacy of Divorce.* New York: Hyperion, 2000.

Wilde, Jerry. *Surviving and Thriving as a Blended Family.* William Neil Publishing, 2000.

Stepparenting

Barnes, Bob. *Winning the Heart of Your Stepchild.* Grand Rapids, Mich.: Zondervan Publishing, 1997.

Burns, Cherie. *Stepmotherhood: How to Survive Wthout Feeling Frustrated, Left Out or Wicked*. New York: Times Books, 1985.

Ford, Judy, and Anna Chase. *Wonderful Ways to Be a Stepparent*. Berkeley, Calif.: Conari Press, 1999.

Lutz, Ericka. *The Complete Idiot's Guide to Stepparenting*. Madison, Wisc.: Alpha Books, 1998.

Mulford, Patricia Greene. *Keys to Successful Stepmothering*. Hauppage, N.Y.: Barron's Educational Series, 1996.

Norwood, Perdita Kirkness, with Teri Wingender. *The Enlightened Stepmother: Revolutionizing the Role*. New York: Avon Books, 1999.

Pickhardt, Carl E. *Keys to Successful Step-Fathering*. New York: Barron's, 1997.

Thoele, Sue Patton. *The Courage to Be a Stepmom: Finding Your Place Without Losing Yourself*. Berkeley, Calif.: Wildcat Canyon Press, 1999.

Co-Parenting

Condrell, Kenneth N., and Linda Lee Small (contributor). *Be a Great Divorced Dad*. New York: St. Martin's Press, 1998.

Klatt, William C. *Live-Away Dads: Staying a Part of Your Children's Lives When They Aren't a Part of Your Home*. New York: Penguin USA, 1999.

Knox, David, and Kermit Leggett (contributor). *The Divorced Dad's Survival Book: How to Stay Connected to Your Kids*. Cambridge, Mass.: Perseus Books, 2000.

Lansky, Vicki. *Divorce Book for Parents: Helping Your Children Cope with Divorce and Its Aftermath*. Minnetonka, Minn.: Book Peddlers, 1996.

Mayer, Gerald S. *The Divorced Dad Dilemma: A Father's Guide to Understanding, Grieving & Growing Beyond the Losses of Divorce*. Phoenix, Ariz.: Motivo Publishing Company, 1997.

McKay, Matthew, Kim Paleg, Patrick Fanning, and Donna Landis. *When Anger Hurts Your Kids: A Parent's Guide*. Oakland, Calif.: New Harbinger Publications, 1996.

Prengel, Serge. *Still a Dad: A Divorced Father's Journey*. New York: Mission Creative Energy, Inc., 1999.

Ricci, Isolina. *Mom's House, Dad's House: Making Two Homes for Your Child*. New York: Simon and Schuster, 1997.

Ross, Julie A., and Judy Corcoran. *Joint Custody with a Jerk: Raising a Child with an Uncooperative Ex*. New York: St. Martin's Press, 1996.

Shami, Nailah. *Taking the High Road: How to Cope With Your Ex-Husband, Maintain Your Sanity, and Raise Your Child in Peace*. New York: Plume, 2000.

Shulman, Diana. *Co-Parenting After Divorce: How to Raise Happy, Healthy Children in Two-Home Families*. Sherman Oaks, Calif.: Winnspeed Press, 1997.

For and About Children and Teens in Stepfamilies

Buchanan, Christy, Eleanor Maccoby, and Sanford Dornbusch. *Adolescents After Divorce*. Cambridge, Mass.: Harvard University Press, 2000.

Carlisle, Erica Celeste. *I Was My Mother's Bridesmaid: Young Adults Talk About Thriving in a Blended Family*. Berkeley, Calif.: Wildcat Canyon Press, 1999.

Doss, Bonnie, and Jennifer Schroeder. *But . . . What About Me! (How It Feels to Be a Kid in Divorce)*. Bookmark Publishing, 1998.

Hoctor, Sarah K. *Changes: My Family and Me*. Washington, D.C.: Child Welfare League of America, 1999.

Holyoke, Nancy. *Help! A Girl's Guide to Divorce and Stepfamilies*. Middleton, Wis.: Pleasant Company Publications, 1999.

Jackson, Alys Swan, Joan Shapiro (contributor), and Lynn
    Rosenfield (contributor). *When Your Parents Split Up: How to
    Keep Yourself Together.* New York: Price Stern Sloan, 1998.

Johnston, Janet, Mitchell Baris, Carla Garrity, and Karen Breunig.
    *Through the Children's Eyes: Healing Stories for Children of
    Divorce.* New York: Free Press, 1997.

Lansky, Vicki, and Jane Prince (illustrator). *It's Not Your Fault,
    Koko Bear: A Read-Together Book for Parents and Young Chil-
    dren During Divorce.* Minnetonka, Minn.: Book Peddlers,
    1998.

Leibowitz, Julie. *Finding Your Place: A Teen Guide to Life in a
    Blended Family* (Divorce Resource Series). New York:
    Rosen Publishing Group, 2000.

Lumpkin, Peggy. *The Stepkin Stories.* Newberg, Oreg.: Book-
    Partners, Inc., 1999.

Monroe, Robin Prince, and Carol Ackelmire (illustrator). *Why
    Don't We Live Together Anymore?* (Comforting Little Hearts
    Series). St. Louis, Mo.: Concordia Publishing House, 1998.

Petersen, P. J., Lynne Cravath (illustrator), and Lucia Monfried
    (editor). *I Hate Weddings* (fiction). New York: Penguin Put-
    nam Books for Young Readers, 2000.

Prilik, Pearl. *Becoming an Adult Stepchild: Adjusting to a Parent's
    New Marriage.* Washington, D.C.: American Psychiatric
    Press, 1998.

Rogers, Fred, and Jim Judkis (illustrator). *Let's Talk About It:
    Divorce.* New York: Philomel Books, 1998.

Rothchild, Gillian. *Dear Mom and Dad: What Kids of Divorce
    Really Want to Say to Their Parents.* New York: Pocket Books,
    1999.

Schneider, Meg F., and Joan Zuckerberg (contributor). *Difficult
    Questions Kids Ask and Are Too Afraid to Ask About Divorce.*
    New York: Fireside, 1996.

Spelman, Cornelia, and Kathy Parkinson (illustrator). *Mama & Daddy Bear's Divorce.* Morton Grove, Ill.: Albert Whitman & Co., 1998.

Staal, Stephanie. *The Love They Lost: Living the Legacy of Our Parents' Divorce.* New York: Dell Publishing Co., 2000.

Stern, Zoe, and Evan Stern. *Divorce Is Not the End of the World: Zoe's and Evan's Coping Guide for Kids.* Berkeley, Calif.: Tricycle Press, 1997.

Stewart, Gail B. *Teens and Divorce* (Lucent Overview Series, Teen Issues). Farmington Hills, Mich.: Lucent Books, 2000.

Thomas, Pat, and Lesley Harker (illustrator). *My Family's Changing: A First Look at Family Break Up.* Hauppage, N.Y. Barron's Educational Series, 1999.

index